—3-D—
Star Maps

-3-D-
Star Maps

RICHARD MONKHOUSE • JOHN COX

HARPER & ROW, PUBLISHERS, New York
Grand Rapids, Philadelphia, St. Louis, San Francisco
London, Singapore, Sydney, Tokyo

This book is published in the United Kingdom by
William Collins Sons & Company Ltd

3-D STAR MAPS Copyright © 1989 Swallow Publishing Ltd
Map design and text © 1989 Richard Monkhouse and John Cox

Edited, designed and produced by
Swallow Books, 260 Pentonville Road,
London N1 9JY

Designer: Stephen Bitti

Editor: Catherine Tilley

Illustrator: Peter Harper

Map annotators: Swanston Graphics, Derby

Typesetter: Opus, Oxford

Printed in Hong Kong by Imago Publishing Limited

FIRST EDITION

Library of Congress Cataloging-in-Publication Data

Cox, John.
    3-D star maps/John Cox and Richard Monkhouse.— 1st ed.
        p.   cm.
    Includes index.
    ISBN 0-06-016131-0 : $
    1. Stars—Charts, diagrams, etc. I. Monkhouse, Richard. II. Title.
    QB6. C79   1989

523.8'022'2—dc20   89-45031

89 90 91 92 93 10 9 8 7 6 5 4 3 2 1

Half title page
M16 (the Eagle Nebula) in the constellation of Serpens Cauda. A composite
photograph made with the U.K. Schmidt Telescope, Australia.

Title page
The "Lagoon" nebula (M8) on the left and the "Trifid" nebula (M20) on the
right. Both nebulae contain recently formed stars, which heat up the gas into
a characteristic red glow. The light from young blue stars in the Trifid
nebula is directly reflected by outlying clouds of cooler dust.

Contents

Introduction

WHEN YOU LOOK at the night sky and watch the Moon, the planets and the stars rising and setting, they seem to do so at a distance just beyond the horizon. But this is an illusion – even the nearest object, the Moon, is many thousands of times further away. When the Moon and the stars pass overhead they seem closer still, as if they were just skimming above the highest clouds. Another illusion is that the Moon and the stars are the same distance away. In fact the most distant stars normally visible are up to 50,000 million times further away from us than the Moon is.

These illusions are produced by your everyday experience of the world around you, where the most distant things you can see are mountains and clouds. They also result from the physical limitations of your eyes, which can judge distance only to a few hundred metres (yards) away. This book makes it possible to see a picture of near space in three dimensions.

The star maps have been generated by computer using astronomical catalogues to plot the position, distance and brightness of each star or other object in space. To keep everything in focus, the depth has to be "logarithmically" compressed, so that distant objects are shown much closer to near objects than they actually are. Being plotted in 3-D creates the effect of some stars receding back into the page and others coming forward out of the page depending on their distance.

How to use this book

The maps in this book show stars and various types of groupings of stars. There are many different kinds of stars, star clusters and other things, like gas clouds. Some of these different "object-types" are represented individually on the maps, and the chapters at the beginning of the book describe what these objects are, how they are measured, and outline some theories about how they are formed and behave. Parts of these chapters are rather technical: the best thing is to start with the maps and work backwards!

The maps are in three main sections. The "Bright Star" maps show objects that can be seen with the naked eye: they picture how the night sky appears to you. The "Near Star" maps show stars that are much closer to the Sun than the stars you normally see, but that are mostly not bright enough to be seen without a telescope. The "Galaxy" maps show the massive groupings of stars that make up the bulk of the observable universe, which are too far away to be seen without a telescope. The map in the centre of the book shows our own galaxy, the Milky Way.

Each map is shown in two forms: in 3-D and in black and white. The black and white maps identify the objects in the 3-D maps, which are printed in red and green and have to be viewed through the red and green glasses found at the back of this book in order to get the "stereoscopic" effect.

At first it may take a moment before you "see" the depth or third dimension of the maps (the older you are, the longer it is likely to take!). Start with one of the maps in the Near Star series as these are easiest to see properly. Open the book squarely in front of you on a table, and look at it from arm's length. View the image under a good light: daylight is best. You will find it is easier to see those objects that go back into the page than those that come out in front. Some maps, and some objects, are more difficult than others. Do not try to "see" every map and every object straight away. The important thing is not to strain for the illusion: the 3-D effect works best when both eyes and brain are relaxed, and it gets easier all the time.

The three series of star maps

With the exception of our local star, the Sun, most stars are so far away that only the brightest can be seen with the naked eye. These are called "naked-eye objects", and are represented in the Bright Star Maps. How bright a star appears to be depends on three things: how dark the sky is; how bright the star is; and how far away it is. These maps show the sky as it looks on a dark and clear night, away from city lights, around the time of the new Moon. Most naked-eye stars are between ten and 1,000 times as bright as the Sun, and between 10 and 3,000 light years away, so the Bright Star Maps depict "middle space". They also show other kinds of astronomical objects, such as star clusters, gas clouds, and galaxies, that are bright enough to be seen with the naked eye or with a small pair of binoculars.

The Near Star Maps depict stars that are 4–80 light years away. This is a long way by our understanding of distance (the nearest star beyond the Sun, Proxima Centauri, is more than 250,000 times further from the Sun than the Earth is), but in astronomical terms it is very close. These maps represent "near space", and most of the stars on them are

The Milky Way in the direction of Sagittarius. The dark areas are dense

much dimmer than the Sun. The "average" near star has only one-fifteenth of the Sun's brightness and many are dimmer still. Very few are bright enough to be seen without telescopes, so these maps give an indication of what near space is really like.

Finally there are the Galaxy Maps, which show a few thousand of the nearer and brighter galaxies beyond our own galaxy, the Milky Way. These objects are enormously bright in themselves, but most of them are too far away to be seen without a telescope, and are located in "far space" thousands and millions of light years away.

Looking at the black and white maps shows what the objects are and where they are found in the night sky. Looking at the 3-D maps shows how far away they are in relation to each other, and from us. All the maps use a system of symbols that indicate firstly what type of star or object it is and secondly, by the size of the symbol, how bright or near it is.

Young stars are formed in gas clouds. The young stars heat up the remains of the cloud so that it shines with its own red light. The hottest and brightest of the young stars shine with a blue light which is reflected by outlying regions of cold interstellar dust and gas. These nebulae lie close to the Lagoon nebula, Sagittarius.

What are the stars ?

*S*TARS ARE MASSIVE, brightly shining spheres of gas, which radiate energy, particularly as light, from a nuclear fusion process inside them. Most of what is "known" about the way stars form, what goes on inside them, and what happens to them in the end, is theory and speculation. Some of these theories can be tested, and are based on nuclear physics, mathematics and the study of the outward behaviour of the stars themselves. This includes observation of our Sun, which is the only star near enough to be studied in detail. However, the Sun is too bright to be examined with conventional instruments, so this is done with specialized equipment.

> Never look directly at the Sun with a telescope or a pair of binoculars – you could be blinded.

Stars are believed to form when part of a cloud of dust and gas (mainly molecular hydrogen) splits off and starts to fall in on itself under the attraction of its own gravity. What it is that starts this happening is not understood, but it probably involves gravity disturbances and pressure waves. Once this process has started in a sufficiently massive cloud of gas, the shrinking material will turn into a star. As the material falls in on itself it generates a great amount of heat, which triggers off a nuclear reaction. The first major reaction (hydrogen turning into helium) starts in the core of the collapsing star, where the pressure and temperature are highest. The energy produced replaces the energy lost in radiation (mostly as heat, visible light and ultra-violet light), and stops the star collapsing further.

This reaction is often compared to that of a hydrogen bomb, but what happens in a star is actually very different. The amount of energy produced by a single fusion of two hydrogen atoms into one helium atom is tiny, and the rate at which these reactions occur in stars is very slow. If the reactions were averaged out among the whole mass of the Sun, the energy production of a cubic metre ($1\frac{1}{5}$ cubic yards) would be about one-quarter of a watt. It would take 240 cubic metres (280 cubic yards) of such material (enough to fill a medium-sized swimming pool) to run a 60-watt light bulb. The reason why stars are in fact so bright and so hot is because they are almost unimaginably huge. The Sun is a small star, but it is still 1,392,000km (865,000 miles) in diameter. Although it is burning at a slow rate, its overall energy output totals 380 million, million, million million watts.

The fusion of hydrogen into helium is the slowest and longest running of the reactions a star can produce. Stars in this condition are known as "dwarf stars", or "main sequence stars" after their position on a commonly used diagram called the Hertzsprung-Russell diagram, which plots their brightness against their surface temperature. How long the initial reaction lasts, how fast it runs, and how brightly the star shines depend on its initial mass or quantity of matter. (We measure the mass of stars against the mass of our own Sun, which therefore is 1 solar mass.)

The more massive the star, the faster the reaction runs, and the brighter it shines. For instance, a star of 1 solar mass will remain on the main sequence for about 9,000 million years. The Sun is estimated to be around 4,500 million years old (one-quarter of the estimated elapsed age of the universe), so it has some time left to run. A high-mass star of 10 solar masses will radiate energy at about 6,000 times the rate of the Sun, and will move away from the main sequence in less than 20 million years. Stars of 0.7 solar masses and below are expected to remain on the main sequence for longer than the elapsed age of the universe, and radiate energy five to 1,000 times as slowly as the Sun.

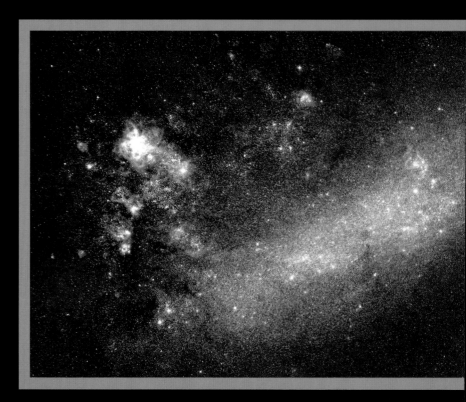

Star colour

It is the temperature of the star's surface that determines the dominant colour of the light it radiates, so that stars with the hottest surface temperature radiate most strongly on the wavelengths of blue light and stars of the coolest surface temperature radiate most strongly on the wavelengths of red light. The effect is similar to what happens to a poker heated in a fire: the poker begins to glow red at first, and as it heats up it passes through yellow, and eventually reaches white. This is about the limit for a poker, but the much hotter flame of a welding torch will burn with a blue light (do not look directly!).

Most active stars are in a balance between the gravity attraction of their material, which is attempting to make the star contract, and the pressure of the gas (heated up by nuclear reactions), which is trying to make the star expand. However, with the completion of one chain of reactions, the rate at which energy is generated slows down, and the star starts collapsing. The increased density of heavier elements at the core creates higher temperatures, and triggers new and more complicated reactions. With each new reaction the rate of energy production rises again, and a new balance is found. The core becomes denser, the new reactions run faster, and the outer layers of the star expand. As they expand, they cool off, changing the colour of the radiated light towards red. Although the surface

At a distance of 50 kpc (160,000 light years) the Large Magellanic Cloud is the nearest galaxy to our own. In February 1987 a supernova explosion was observed, and was briefly visible to the naked eye in the southern sky.

Below Supernova 1987a (detail) is under intense study. It appears to have become a neutron star.

ps, the overall size of the surface is much
al light output is larger, and the star
ed-orange or yellow giant.
 star between one and five times the mass
al reaction of which it is capable is the
 into carbon in a shell around its core. At
 is a red giant, with a diameter perhaps
he Sun. Any area of the star's surface will
 tenth of the light of the same area of the
 because the surface area of the star is so
ill be putting out up to 1,000 times as much

The late reactions of a red giant are fast running and unstable. As a red giant of low mass approaches the end of its active life, the outer layers of the star may expand in a spherical shell of gas, which eventually drifts off into space. The inert carbon core is left behind to radiate away its heat, first as a white dwarf 100–1,000 times less bright than the Sun, and then gradually cooling through yellow, orange, and red, to end up as a cold "black dwarf".

High-mass stars can produce sufficiently dense and high temperature cores to run beyond the fusion of helium into carbon, and successive reactions may fuse carbon into magnesium, magnesium into neon, and neon into iron. The fusion of iron into heavier elements does not produce energy, but consumes it instead. What happens to a high-mass star at the end of its life is not understood very clearly, but it appears that those with a core rich in iron may finally explode in a "supernova" outburst.

In some cases the star may simply reduce itself to a great cloud of gas and dust. In others the core remains intact as a tiny neutron star, collapsed to a diameter of 20–30km (12–20 miles), spinning at thirty times a second or faster. Very massive cores may collapse even further, creating a body so dense and gravitationally attractive that no light can escape: a "black hole".

When a star blows up in a supernova explosion, chains of reaction take place, some of them producing heavy elements. These heavy elements join the gas and dust in space from which more stars are made. As the material from stars is recycled in this way, the initial mix of elements gets richer, so that more recently formed stars contain more metals than older stars. Some of this dust ends up in planets, such as our own iron- and heavy element- rich Earth.

Star brightness

The brightness of a celestial object is called its "luminosity", but in astronomical catalogues and star maps the older word "magnitude" is used. This use of the word comes from the Greeks, who called the brightest stars "stars of the first magnitude", stars not quite so bright "stars of the second magnitude", and so on.

How bright a star appears to the observer on Earth is called its "apparent visual magnitude", and depends on two things: how bright it really is (its intrinsic luminosity) and how far away it is. Using the same system, the intrinsic luminosity (how bright the star really is) is called its "absolute magnitude". The absolute magnitude of a star is what its apparent magnitude would be if it was observed from a distance of 10 parsecs (each parsec is equivalent to about 3.262 light years).

Some stars appear brighter than stars of the first magnitude, and so are measured through zero and into negative figures. This means that on the scale of magnitude the dimmest objects have the highest positive values and the brightest objects have the highest negative values. Each step in magnitude represents a two and a half times increase in brightness, so that five magnitudes refers to a difference of 100 times the brightness.

Here are some examples: Vega, the bright star in Lyra, has an apparent visual magnitude (V) of +0.03; the slightly brighter star Arcturus, in Bootes, is V–0.06, the brightest star in the night sky; Sirius (the bright star in Canis Major) is V–1.46. From our position on Earth the star with the brightest apparent visual magnitude is the Sun (V–26.7). But at a distance of 10 parsecs the Sun would have an apparent visual magnitude of only +4.8, and this is, therefore, its absolute magnitude. The star Rigel, the blue star in the western foot of Orion, has an absolute magnitude of –7.0, making it 50,000 times more luminous than the Sun.

The faintest star that can normally be picked out with the naked eye under good, steady conditions has an apparent visual magnitude of approximately +6.5. There are about 8,000 stars down to this magnitude limit, which is sometimes called the "limit of naked-eye seeing". The limit on the stars shown in the Bright Star Maps is set at V+6.2. However, someone with good eyesight observing from the clear, thin air of a mountain should be able to see well beyond this limit, perhaps to V+7.0 and further.

Spectral types and luminosity classes

The best-known colour spectrum is the rainbow. Another familiar spectrum is the band of coloured light produced when sunlight passes through a triangular glass prism. In these spectra "white light" is seen broken into the rainbow colours violet, blue, green, yellow, orange and red. All sunlight (the Sun is a star after all) can be broken up in this way, and if the light from an individual star is collected in a telescope and passed through an arrangement of

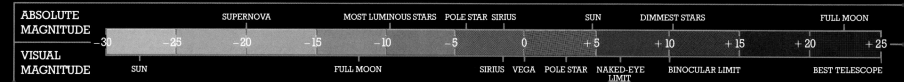

ABSOLUTE MAGNITUDE				SUPERNOVA		MOST LUMINOUS STARS	POLE STAR	SIRIUS		SUN		DIMMEST STARS			FULL MOON	
	–30	–25	–20	–15	–10	–5		0	+5		+10		+15		+20	+25
VISUAL MAGNITUDE	SUN				FULL MOON			SIRIUS	VEGA	POLE STAR	NAKED-EYE LIMIT	BINOCULAR LIMIT			BEST TELESCOPE	

lenses and prisms (called a spectroscope) the continuous shading of the colour spectrum is found to be crossed by dark lines. These are known as "absorption lines" because they are created by the elements in the gas at the surface of the star absorbing light, with each element creating a shadow at a particular wavelength. The strength and sharpness of each absorption line depends on the abundance of the element, and on the temperature and pressure of the gas.

The surface temperature of the star is calculated from the appearance of absorption lines particularly sensitive to temperature. It is the surface temperature that determines how energetically it is radiating light and the dominant frequency (colour wavelength) of the light radiated. This is recorded as the star's "spectral type". The main spectral types are arranged in a sequence that runs from "hot" blue "O" types down to "cool" red "M" types. The sequence is easily remembered by the phrase "Oh Be A Fine Girl Kiss Me", corresponding to the classes O (blue and ultra-violet), B (blue), A (green), F (appears white), G (yellow), K (orange), M (red). Each class is divided into ten sub-classes, from 0 to 9.

The human eye is not sensitive to colour at low levels of light, so only the brightest stars appear coloured. These colours are subtle, but perfectly apparent if you look for them: Betelgeuse (M2) appears red; Aldeberan (K5) appears orange; Sirius (A1) appears green; the Sun (G2) appears yellow (don't look directly).

Analysis of pressure-sensitive absorption lines indicates the density of the gas at the surface of the star. This shows whether the star is a comparatively dense, main sequence star, or a more expanded and diffuse giant or supergiant.

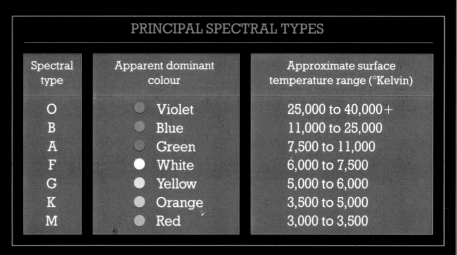

PRINCIPAL SPECTRAL TYPES		
Spectral type	Apparent dominant colour	Approximate surface temperature range (°Kelvin)
O	Violet	25,000 to 40,000+
B	Blue	11,000 to 25,000
A	Green	7,500 to 11,000
F	White	6,000 to 7,500
G	Yellow	5,000 to 6,000
K	Orange	3,500 to 5,000
M	Red	3,000 to 3,500

How expanded the star is determines how much surface area there is to radiate light. The potential luminosity of the star is recorded as one of five main "luminosity classes", referred to by the Roman numerals I to V, so that I (subdivided into Ia–O, Ia, Iab, and Ib) are supergiants, II are bright giants, III are giants, IV are subgiants, and V are main sequence stars (or "dwarf" stars).

Most of the stars in the immediate neighbourhood of the Sun are main sequence stars of the K and M types. Although they are very close, this means that their intrinsic luminosity is too low for them to be seen with the naked eye. Most of the naked-eye stars are either hot blue main sequence stars, such as Spica (B1 V), or else giant or supergiant stars, such as Betelgeuse (M2 Ia). These stars are comparatively rare in numerical terms, but their enormous luminosity enables them to be seen at great distances. A notable exception is Sirius, which is an A1 V star at 8.7 light years distance, making it the second brightest star in the sky after the Sun (8.3 light minutes away).

Measuring distance

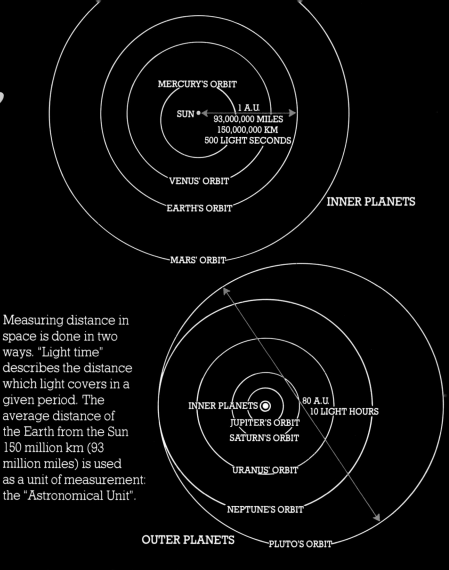

*A*STRONOMICAL DISTANCES are so great they are almost impossible to imagine. Several different units of distance are used in astronomy, of which the most familiar is the light year. This is the distance that light, travelling at 299,792km (186,282 miles) per second, covers in the course of a year. From this comes a more general idea of "light time", according to which the Moon is one and a half light seconds away, because it takes this long for the light to reach us from the Moon. It takes light from the Sun eight minutes to reach Earth, five hours to reach Pluto (the outermost planet of our solar system) and more than four years to reach the nearest star, Proxima Centauri.

Astronomical unit

Distances inside the solar system are measured in astronomical units. The unit is close to the average distance of the Earth from the Sun, which means that 1 astronomical unit (A.U.) is roughly equivalent to 150 million km (93 million miles) in distance.

Parsecs

If photographs of stars are taken at one point in the Earth's one-year orbit around the Sun, and the same stars are photographed six months later, when the two photographs are compared the position of the nearest stars will appear to have shifted a little. This effect is due to "parallax", and

Measuring distance in space is done in two ways. "Light time" describes the distance which light covers in a given period. The average distance of the Earth from the Sun 150 million km (93 million miles) is used as a unit of measurement: the "Astronomical Unit".

using it as a technique of measurement is called the "parallax method".

To see what parallax is, look at what happens to your finger when you hold it out in front of you and look at it with each eye in turn. Viewed like this, the finger seems to shift from side to side against the background of distant objects. This is an effect of parallax, and comes about when a

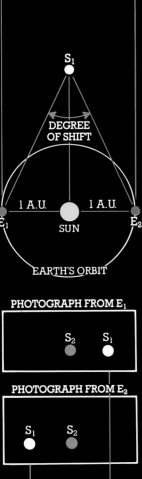

TO DISTANT STAR S₂

S_1

DEGREE
OF SHIFT

1 A.U.   1 A.U.

E_1 E_2

SUN

EARTH'S ORBIT

PHOTOGRAPH FROM E_1

S_2 S_1

PHOTOGRAPH FROM E_2

S_1 S_2

DEGREE OF SHIFT

COMPARING UNITS OF DISTANCE

1 Astronomical unit

149,597,870 km 92,955,807 miles	Distance light travels in 499 seconds

1 Light year

63,240 Astronomical units 9,460,500,000,000 km 5,878,500,000,000 miles	Distance light travels in one year

1 Parsec

3.2616 Light years 206,265 Astronomical units 30,857,000,000,000 km 19,174,000,000,000 miles	Three-quarters of the distance to Proxima Centauri

1 kpc (kiloparsec)	1,000 pc
1 Mpc (megaparsec)	1,000 kpc
	1,000,000 pc
1 Gpc (gigaparsec)	1,000 Mpc
	1,000,000 kpc
	1,000,000,000 pc

"Parsecs" are derived from the way the great distances between stars are actually measured. The diagram (not to scale!) shows how the images of a near star and a far star change position when photographed from each side of the Earth's orbit.

nearby object is seen from two points of view, in this case from a "baseline" of two eyes about 6–7cm (2½in.) apart. Seeing a nearby object in focus involves converging your eyes slightly in order to bring the two images into one. You hardly notice the way you do this, but it is one of the most important ways you "see" the distance of nearby objects. Once objects are more than a few hundred metres (yards)

away, the baseline of the eyes is too small to produce parallax, and you rely on experience and expectation to gauge how far away things are.

Six month's orbit takes the Earth to the opposite side of the Sun, and creates a baseline 2A.U. wide. This baseline is wide enough to use parallax for measuring distance in space: the distance an object would have to be to show one arcsecond (one-sixtieth of one-sixtieth degree of arc) of parallax when observed sideways on from a baseline 150 million km (93 million miles: 1A.U.) long is called a parsec (pc). The parsec is a large-scale unit, and it is used in the keys to the maps.

Even among the nearest stars the apparent shifts in position produced by parallax are very small, and the instruments used to take the photographs and measure the images have to be extremely precise. Unfortunately, the distortions induced by the Earth's atmosphere and the optics of the telescope limit the accuracy of ground-based observations and the results become increasingly unreliable for stars further than 100pc.

However, there are enough stars whose distance can be measured in this way to give a broad sample of different star types, allowing astronomers to calculate the absolute magnitude of particular star types. The distance to most of the stars nearer than 200pc shown in this book have been calculated by the parallax method.

Luminosity class

By comparing luminosity class with spectral type it is possible to estimate the intrinsic luminosity of a particular star. By comparing how bright it appears to be (its apparent magnitude) with how bright it really is (its absolute magnitude), a simple calculation suggests how far away it is (observed brightness decreases according to the square of the distance). The distances to stars further than 200pc shown in this book have been estimated by this method.

Standard candles

The maximum and minimum amounts of light produced by some types of variable star (see page 22) appear to be very similar from one example to another, and to be closely related to the rate of their variation. Astronomers are fairly confident about the intrinsic luminosities of these star types, some of which are bright enough to be picked out in nearby galaxies. By comparing absolute magnitude with apparent magnitude it is possible to estimate the distance to these stars, and so to the galaxy in which they are found. Stars used in this way are called standard candles, and this method will have been used to estimate the distances to some of the nearer galaxies shown on the Galaxy Maps.

Redshift

If you listen to a motor car passing at speed, the engine note changes pitch as it passes. While the car is approaching the motor makes a high note, as it passes the note suddenly drops, and as it speeds away, the sound continues at a lower pitch. This is known as a "doppler effect" (after the Austrian physicist C.J. Doppler), and is caused by the relative motion of the listener and the sound source. Thinking of sound as a series of waves, with higher notes produced by shorter waves, the distance between wave crests is shortened as the sound source approaches because each new wave is produced a little nearer the

listener, causing them to "pile up" in front of the sound source. This reduces the effective distance between waves and so raises the pitch of the sound. When the sound source is travelling away this effect is reversed, and the wavelength is stretched out, producing a lower note.

A similar effect can be observed in wavelengths of light. When a star is travelling away from our own Sun, or when a galaxy is travelling away from our own galaxy, the wavelengths of light reach us stretched out. As the wavelengths of light at the red end of the colour spectrum are about twice the length of the wavelengths at the blue end, movement away from the observer has the effect of moving light into the red end of the colour spectrum. This effect is known as "redshift" and is used to estimate how fast an object in space is travelling away from an observer.

Because the universe as a whole is believed to be expanding, with the more distant galaxies travelling away faster than the nearer ones, the speed at which galaxies are travelling is used to estimate their distance from us. Redshifts are an unreliable way of calculating the distance of nearer galaxies because local movements mean that some are travelling away faster than average, while others are actually moving nearer. Beyond a certain distance (perhaps 10 Mpc; 10,000,000 parsecs), these local movements start to be lost in the much larger movement of an expanding universe, making redshift a useful method of estimating distance. (Not all astronomers agree that the assumptions behind the calculation of distance from redshift are correct.)

With the exception of about a hundred of the nearest ones, the distances to galaxies shown on the maps have been derived from their redshift.

The star maps

Terrestrial coordinates
are projected on to the
inside of an imaginary
"Celestial Sphere".

NORTH CELESTIAL POLE

*E*ACH SERIES OF MAPS – the Bright Star, Near Star and Galaxy – is introduced by two small scale maps showing the principal celestial objects of that series and indicating the particular maps in which they are found. There is also a map of the centre of the Milky Way.

The positions of the stars, galaxies and other objects in space are defined on the maps with symbols, using grids that indicate "how far up" an object is and "how far round" it is. These grid systems are called coordinates.

The most familiar sets of coordinates are the imaginary lines of longitude and latitude that divide up the surface of the "terrestial sphere", Earth. "Lines of equal longitude" start at the poles and divide up the globe from top to bottom like the segments of an orange. "Lines of equal latitude" divide up the globe the other way, like the stripes on a seaman's jumper.

SOUTH CELESTIAL POLE

Celestial coordinates

In a system of celestial coordinates (the green grids used in the Bright and Near Star Maps series) terrestrial coordinates are projected on to the inside of an imaginary "celestial sphere", which surrounds Earth like a shell. Lines of equal terrestrial longitude become lines of "right ascension", and lines of terrestrial latitude become lines of "equal declination". The point overhead at the terrestrial north pole becomes the north celestial pole, the point overhead at the

terrestial south pole becomes the south celestial pole, and the band of sky that lies over the terrestrial equator becomes the celestial equator.

The zero-point of right ascension is fixed by the position of the Sun as it crosses the celestial equator at the time of the spring equinox in the Northern Hemisphere. (The spring equinox is one of the two occasions each year when day and night are of equal length everywhere on Earth.)

Degrees of right ascension run eastwards round the celestial equator, and are marked off into 360 degrees, a system we have inherited from the Babylonians. Another way of dividing the equator is into twenty-four hours, as this is approximately the time it takes (actually twenty-three hours and fifty-six minutes) for the whole circle of the heavens to pass overhead. This book uses the twenty-four hour system.

Degrees of declination are divided into the 90° north and south of the celestial equator, with the north celestial pole at 90°N and the south celestial pole at 90°S. The position of the Sun at the time of the spring equinox, right ascension 0°, declination 0°, is called the "First Point of Aries". This is also the starting point for another set of sky coordinates called "ecliptic coordinates".

Ecliptic coordinates

If it were possible to see the stars in the daytime, the Sun would seem to be moving slowly eastwards, about 1° every twenty-four hours, against a background of the fixed stars. The track of the Sun is called the "ecliptic" as this is the path on which eclipses of the Sun and Moon are observed. The ecliptic represents the plane in which the Earth is orbiting the Sun. The spinning Earth is not set square in the plane of the Earth's orbit round the Sun, but is at an angle of 23½°. This means that the plane of the ecliptic (generated by the Earth's orbit round the Sun), and the plane of the celestial equator (generated by the axis of the spinning Earth) don't coincide, but intersect at the same angle of 23½°. The ecliptic is divided into 360° of "celestial longitude".

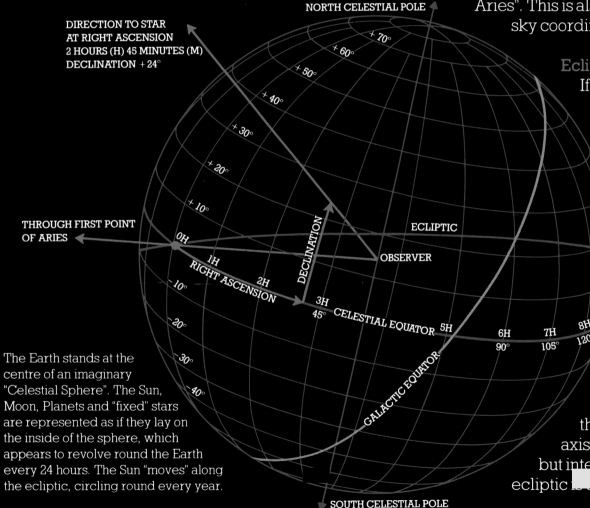

DIRECTION TO STAR
AT RIGHT ASCENSION
2 HOURS (H) 45 MINUTES (M)
DECLINATION +24°

NORTH CELESTIAL POLE

+ 70°
+ 60°
+ 50°
+ 40°
+ 30°
+ 20°
+ 10°

THROUGH FIRST POINT
OF ARIES

0H
1H
RIGHT ASCENSION
2H
-10°
-20°
-30°
-40°

DECLINATION

ECLIPTIC

OBSERVER

3H
45° CELESTIAL EQUATOR 5H

6H
90°
7H
105°
8H
120°

GALACTIC EQUATOR

SOUTH CELESTIAL POLE

The Earth stands at the centre of an imaginary "Celestial Sphere". The Sun, Moon, Planets and "fixed" stars are represented as if they lay on the inside of the sphere, which appears to revolve round the Earth every 24 hours. The Sun "moves" along the ecliptic, circling round every year.

There are 90° of "celestial latitude" (not shown) to each of the ecliptic poles.

Not only is the Earth spinning on its own axis, but the axis of the spin is performing a slow loop, called a gyration. This gyration is rather like the secondary looping in a spinning top, with the Earth taking 25,780 years to complete a circuit. This means that the celestial poles are not fixed, but describe a slow circuit through the northern and southern skies, taking the celestial equator and the whole system of celestial coordinates with them. As a result, the First Point of Aries moves 1° westwards along the ecliptic in seventy-two years. Because of these movements, sky maps are fixed for some particular period of time, known as an epoch. In the case of the maps in this book, the coordinates are set for Epoch AD2000.

Galactic coordinates

The third system of coordinates used in this book are the galactic. The zero point of these coordinates is set by the position of the centre of our own galaxy, the Milky Way. The Milky Way is shaped like a large, flat dish, with most of the very luminous stars found near the central plane of the dish. A line drawn along the centre of this plane becomes the galactic equator. The centre of the galaxy is identified with a powerful source of radio energy (there is too much dust to see it from Earth) known as Sagittarius A, which may be generated by a black hole. A point close to this position in Sagittarius becomes galactic longitude 0°.

This long exposure photograph has been taken towards the centre of our own galaxy. Clouds of stars and dark, obscuring clouds of dust and gas shut out any optical view of a powerful source of radio energy, Sagittarius A,

NORTH GALACTIC POLE (+90° GALACTIC LATITUDE)
IN THE DIRECTION OF COMA BERENICES

0°

90°

N

270°

PLANE OF GALAXY (0° GALACTIC LATITUDE)

The Milky Way is a
spiral galaxy 30kpc in
diameter, with most
outlying stars ranged
in "arms". The Sun is in
the Cygnus Arm,
10 kpc from the centre.

180°

SOUTH GALACTIC POLE (-90° GALACTIC LATITUDE IN THE DIRECTION OF SCULPTOR)

Degrees of galactic longitude are marked eastwards from 0° to 360°, so that the direction away from the centre, towards Gemini, Auriga, and the edge of the galaxy, is given by galactic longitude 180°. Degrees up and down ("above" and "below" the plane of the galaxy), are given as 90° of galactic latitude north or south, with the north galactic pole in the direction of Coma Berenices, and the south galactic pole in the direction of Sculptor.

The galactic equator is shown on the Bright Star and Near Star Maps in pink. The Centre of the Galaxy Map and the Galaxy Maps are drawn up on galactic coordinates proper.

What the map symbols mean

ALL THE MAPS in this book use a system of symbols, described below, to indicate what type of object in space is being shown. On the Bright Star Maps and Galaxy Maps the varying size of the symbols represents the apparent magnitude of the object – the larger the symbol, the brighter the object appears in the sky – corresponding to the way we see the night sky. The Near Star Maps, however, show stars that are normally invisible to the naked eye, and on these maps the symbol size refers to their distance away from us (the larger the symbol, the closer the object). The overall range of apparent visual magnitude is so great, and the apparent visual magnitude of the majority of nearby stars is so low, that representation of visual magnitude would make these maps difficult to "read".

The Sun is a star, and the Earth is one of the planets in orbit around it. Sunlight delivers 1 kilowatt of energy to a square metre (yard) of the Earth's surface: this energy is the power source for all of Earth's life-systems. Other stars may have planets, but the planets of even the nearest stars will be too distant to be seen.

Stars ●
The majority of stars appear to be single objects and in a relatively stable condition. When individual stars are studied in detail it turns out that a minority have at least a companion star (see Multiple stars), while a majority will display a degree of variability. For instance, the Sun displays slight variations in output, and is accompanied by a number of planetary companions, of which the giant planet Jupiter is sometimes given as an example of a "brown star". (A brown star is an object whose mass is not sufficient to generate a main sequence reaction, but which nevertheless is producing a small amount of light, probably generated by its own forces of gravitational contraction.) From the viewpoint of some other star, using the technology presently available to us, Jupiter would be totally invisible, and the Sun's slight variability would probably escape notice.

At least some of the stars marked on the star maps as stable stars without companions are, in fact, much more complicated objects than they appear to be at present.

Multiple stars ◉
Many nearby stars appear to consist of two stars orbiting around a common centre of gravity. Some stars are more complicated still, with three or more components. As the

stars in these systems go into a phase of expansion or contraction, they tend to rob each other of material. This can change their mass and composition, and affects the way they evolve.

Variable stars

Many stars show significant variations in brightness. There are many different types of variable star, but they can be divided into two main groups, "extrinsic" and "intrinsic" variables.

Extrinsic variables occur when the star actually consists of two stars in close orbit. As one star passes in front of the other the observed brightness decreases, and when it moves clear of its companion, so that both are open to view, the observed brightness increases.

Intrinsic variables are stars whose variations in brightness are the result of an internal process in the star itself. These stars are usually in a late and complicated stage in their life, when the balance of the opposing forces of gravity and gas pressure has become a dynamic see-saw, with the star expanding and contracting and producing a pulsing of light.

Multiple variables

Where a star is marked as both multiple and variable, it may be one of three types. In the first type both stars may be stable and showing a simple case of extrinsic variability. In the second type one of the components of the multiple star may be an

intrinsic variable. In the third type one star may be stealing gas from a companion, burning it off in a surge of brightness, and then repeating the process.

Open clusters

Open clusters are comparatively small groupings of new stars, typically 20–500 stars grouped in a region that is about 5–20pc across. They are found in the plane of the Milky Way, and observation of open clusters in other galaxies suggests that most of them are found in the outer limbs of the spiral arms.

Open clusters are thought to be groups of new stars that have recently formed, and that have not yet drifted apart.

Globular clusters

These are dense populations of old stars, with 50,000 to a million stars concentrated into the centre of a space 5–50pc in diameter. At the centre the density may reach several thousand stars to the cubic parsec, creating a strong and complicated gravitational field.

Globular clusters are made up of old stars that were formed early in the life of the galaxy: there are about 120 globular clusters visible in our own galaxy. Because they are distributed in a halo surrounding the centre of the galaxy, lying at a typical distance of about 20kpc, it seems that only a few globular clusters are hidden behind the dust clouds that obscure the centre of the Milky Way.

Above There are about 120 globular clusters and they surround the galaxy in elliptical orbits independent of the plane of the Milky Way. Each cluster may contain up to a million very old stars, stars formed in the early life of the galaxy before the development of the galactic disc.

Right The Pleiades (sometimes called the "Seven Sisters") is an open cluster in Taurus. It is a group of stars recently formed in the same gas cloud. Remaining traces of the cloud reflect the light of the hotter B-type stars. The less bright stars are mostly A and F types.

Light from Antares (the red supergiant in Scorpius) floods the bottom left of the photograph, and produces a red-brown fringe of reflection nebula. Sigma (right) appears in a red emission nebula. A blue reflection nebula surrounds the blue star Rho Ophiuchus (top). The globular cluster M4 appears cream (bottom).

Gas clouds ☐

Gas and dust clouds are often known by the term "nebulae", Latin for "misty things". In the eighteenth century this was a term given to any indistinct and luminous object that was not a star. A list of just over a hundred nebulae was drawn up by the French astronomer Charles Messier in order to distinguish them from his primary interest, comets, which also appear nebulous. The Messier list included many objects that turned out to be star clusters and galaxies. Nowadays the term nebulae is only used to describe various kinds of dust and gas cloud. These are divided into "bright nebulae" and "dark nebulae". Both may consist of similar mixtures of dust and gas, but dark nebulae have no stars to excite or illuminate them, and are seen only as dark clouds obscuring the light from the stars beyond.

Bright nebulae are divided into "bright emission nebulae" and "bright reflection nebulae". One kind of bright emission nebula, such as M42 (the M signifies that it was listed by Messier), is a gas cloud, part of which has clumped together to form stars. The still-forming stars excite the surrounding gas to the point where the gas radiates light.

Planetary nebulae (and supernova remnants) ⟨ ⟩

Planetary nebulae and supernova remnants are types of bright emission nebulae that are formed at the end of a star's lifetime. A planetary nebula is an expanding shell of ionized and radiant gas blown out from a star, usually in peaceful transition from red giant to white dwarf, and a supernova remnant is the expanding shell of a star gone supernova, a star in transition to a neutron star or black hole, or blown up entirely.

When a star blows up it produces an enormous surge of light, making it suddenly and temporarily up to 100 million times as bright as it was before. This can make the star visible where formerly it could not be seen, to the extent that it might even become visible in daylight. This happened in the (super)nova of AD1054. A star that suddenly appeared in this way was once thought to be a new star, a "stella nova". This is ironic, since a star that becomes a (super)nova is actually dying.

Galaxies on Bright Star Maps ◗; on Galaxy Maps ◯

Apart from individual stars and planets, the most visible feature in the night sky is the cloudy band of light that is the Milky Way galaxy. Observation of the Milky Way is made difficult by huge clouds of dust and gas, but it is thought that from distant space it would look similar to the "nearby" galaxy M31 in Andromeda. The Milky Way is estimated to contain 1 million, million solar masses, most of which cannot be observed but which may be in the form of black holes, elementary particles and brown stars, reaching out beyond the observable limits of the galaxy.

Our galaxy is just one of millions of galaxies that exist in all directions. Many appear to have flattened spiral structures like our own galaxy, others seem to have no particular structure, being more or less lozenge-shaped clouds of dust and gas known as "elliptical galaxies". Others, such as the nearby satellite galaxies the Magellanic Clouds, show no structure at all, and are therefore known as "irregular" galaxies.

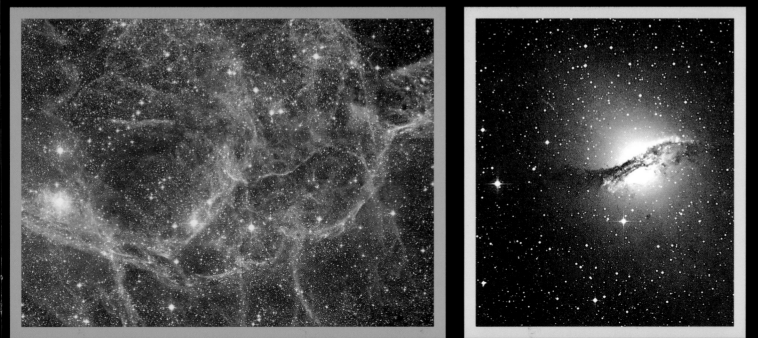

Far left Ten thousand years after the event, a shell of gas still expands from the site of the Vela supernova. Some of this gas will eventually be formed into new stars.

Left The elliptical galaxy Centaurus A is crossed by a curious dust belt, and is a powerful and little understood source of x-ray and radio waves.

Practical observing

THE BEST WAY to recognize the star groups is to look at the night sky with someone who already knows their way around. If you can't do this, then the North and South Circles on pages 30–3 and the Bright Star Maps series can be used to identify the star groups and the brighter nebulae. The planets Venus, Mars, Jupiter and Saturn are easy to confuse with stars. Find out their positions from a newspaper or magazine and then track their movements from night to night.

The easiest method of becoming familiar with the star groups is to start with one or two groups and use these as reference points for the rest. Which groups you use depends on the time of the year. Let us assume that you are going to do your observing about an hour after sunset, when the stars have just started to come out.

Observation in the Northern Hemisphere

At any time of the year, find Ursa Major and then follow a line from the two far stars of the bowl to find Polaris, the north star.

In the middle of spring, start with Leo. This constellation will be rising in the south-east. From Leo, move higher in the sky to find Ursa Major. Locate the bright stars Castor and Pollux in Gemini, sinking into the west. Later in the evening, find Arcturus in Bootes. The position of this star is indicated by the handle of Ursa Major, which points at it

In the middle of summer, start with Ursa Major, high in the western sky. Arcturus is moving into the west. High in the south-east is the bright star Vega in Lyra. Later on in the summer, or later at night, find the three bright stars Vega, Deneb and Altair making up the "summer triangle".

In the middle of autumn the summer triangle is overhead at dusk. The four bright stars that make up the "square of Pegasus"; are climbing in the south-eastern sky. To the north of Pegasus is the "W" shape of Cassiopeia.

In the middle of winter, find the bright smudge of the Pleiades rising from the south east into the south. The bright

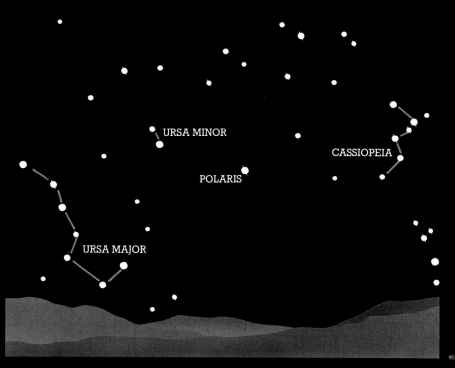

The easiest constellation to find in the northern sky is Ursa Major (the Great Bear). The two stars in the bowl point to Polaris (the Pole Star). On the other side of the pole is the "W" shape of Cassiopeia.

red star Aldeberan lies below it to the east, part of the "V" shape of the Hyades. Rising in the east, below Aldeberan, is the giant constellation of Orion.

Observation in the Southern Hemisphere

At any time of the year find the Southern Cross, circling the pole. In line with the crossbar are the bright stars Agena and Rigel Centaurus (Toliman). Achernar lies on the other side of the pole.

In the middle of spring, Altair in Aquila is high in the northern sky. In the southern sky, the Southern Cross lies to the west of the pole. Between the Southern Cross and Aquila are found Scorpius and Sagittarius. The centre of the galaxy lies in this direction – on a moonless night, note the brightness of the Milky Way.

In summer, Achernar in Eridanus stands above the pole. Orion is rising in the north-eastern sky and blue-green Sirius follows it.

In autumn, Sirius is overhead at dusk. Procyon is north east. Canopus stands over the pole.

In winter, Corvus passes overhead. Spica in Virgo follows. The Southern Cross stands over the pole.

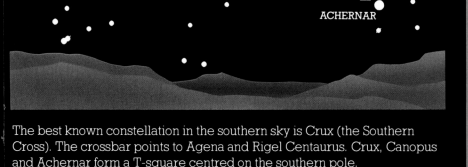

The best known constellation in the southern sky is Crux (the Southern Cross). The crossbar points to Agena and Rigel Centaurus. Crux, Canopus and Achernar form a T-square centred on the southern pole.

This is a "backyard photograph" of Orion (12 secs, f1.7). Photographing stars is a good way to get familar with the night sky. Use a 35mm camera, tripod, cable release and colour slide film.

The bright and near star maps

WHEN WE LOOK at the night sky, the stars appear to lie on the inside of a spherical cover that passes overhead and drops down to a circular ring around the horizon of the flat earth. This imaginary cover is part of an imaginary sphere, the "celestial sphere", surrounding the Earth. Of course, the celestial sphere is not really there and the stars do not lie on it, but the idea of a sphere is a useful one, and star maps are drawn up as if it did exist. This presents the difficulty of representing something that is spherical on a flat piece of paper. All ways of doing this "projection" produce distortions. The projections used in the maps in this book use "Platonic Solids" (convex solids all of whose faces are the same equal-angled shape and whose points lie on the surface of an imaginary sphere) in a way first developed by the American inventor Buckminster Fuller. The Bright Star Maps have been drawn on a twelve-sided figure, the dodecahedron, and the Near Star Maps have been drawn on a six-sided figure, the cube. These maps are drawn in a polar projection from the centre of each face. This projection represents the sphere of the heavens with the smallest amount of distortion possible in the given number of sheets.

The Galaxy Maps have been projected on to an eight-sided figure, the octahedron. Because the area within 15° of the galactic equator is occupied by the Milky Way galaxy itself (the "Plane of Obscuration") and no external galaxies

The Platonic Solids are the bases of the map projections used in this book.

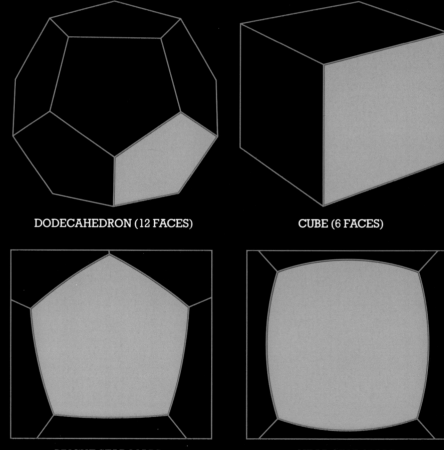

DODECAHEDRON (12 FACES) **CUBE (6 FACES)**

BRIGHT STAR MAPS **NEAR STAR MAPS**

can be seen through it, the centre of projection has been shifted to 50° N or S, so as to minimize distortion among the galaxies that are shown.

Star names

Stars may be named in several ways. Many of the brighter stars have their own individual proper names, for instance Polaris, Sirius and Canopus. All the bright stars have been grouped into particular constellations, and the brighter stars in most constellations have been numbered. In all constellations the brighter stars have been given letters.

Most of the star names and constellations that have survived into the scientific use of the present time have their origin in the Middle East and eastern Mediterranean of the period 2000BC to AD200. The Arabs gave names to many stars, and have handed a large number of these names down to us intact. Some of the Arab names have been superseded by Roman ones, while other names, such as Polaris in Ursa Minor and Acrux in the Southern Cross (Crux), are Latinish names introduced by later astronomers.

In 1603 Johann Bayer devised a system in which the brightest star in a constellation was called "alpha", after the first letter in the Greek alphabet, the second brightest "beta", after the second letter, the third "delta", and so on through the twenty-four letters of the Greek alphabet. This system works well, and is still in use.

A star catalogue by John Flamsteed was published in 1725, which numbered the brighter stars in each constellation, starting from the western side. These numbers are a convenient way of referring to stars that are not quite bright enough to have Bayer letters.

THE GREEK ALPHABET							
Alpha	α	Eta	η	Nu	ν	Tau	τ
Beta	β	Theta	θ	Xi	ξ	Upsilon	υ
Gamma	γ	Iota	ι	Omicron	o	Phi	φ
Delta	δ	Kappa	κ	Pi	π	Chi	χ
Epsilon	ϵ	Lamda	λ	Rho	ρ	Psi	ψ
Zeta	ζ	Mu	μ	Sigma	σ	Omega	ω

The Arabs did not name the most southerly stars because they could not see them, so very few of these stars have proper names. Flamsteed's catalogue also did not reach down to the most southerly stars. Therefore, amateur astronomers in the Southern Hemisphere may find themselves in the odd situation of having only the Bayer system, extended to include the capital and small letters of the Roman alphabet in order to name the stars around the southern celestial pole.

The maps show star names where these are still in use. Bayer letters are given for most of the brighter stars, and some Flamsteed numbers are also shown. Most of the nearer stars shown in the Near Star maps are numbered according to the Catalogue of Nearby Stars (W. Gliese). Clusters, nebulae and galaxies are given Messier numbers and numbers from the New General Catalogue of Non-Stellar Objects.

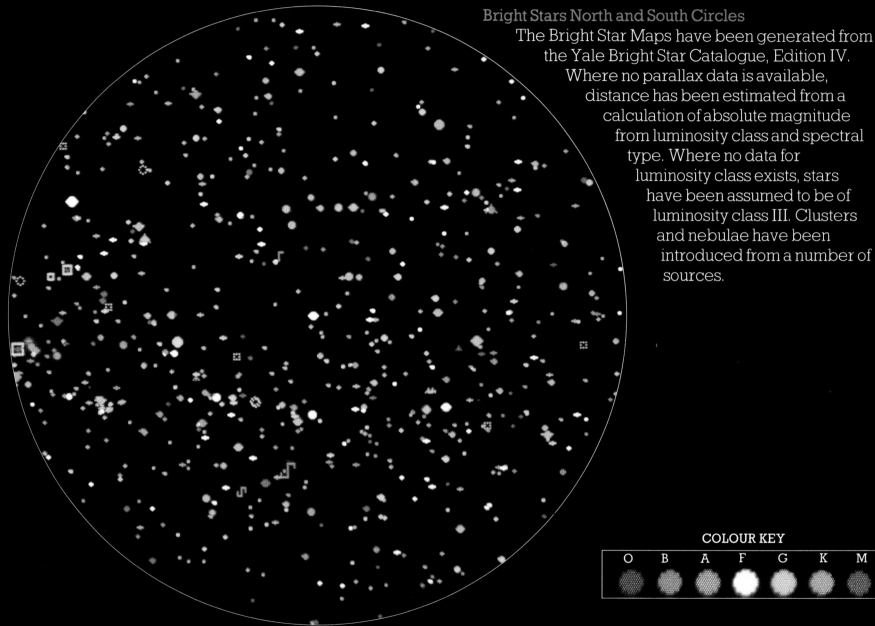

Bright Stars North and South Circles
The Bright Star Maps have been generated from the Yale Bright Star Catalogue, Edition IV. Where no parallax data is available, distance has been estimated from a calculation of absolute magnitude from luminosity class and spectral type. Where no data for luminosity class exists, stars have been assumed to be of luminosity class III. Clusters and nebulae have been introduced from a number of sources.

COLOUR KEY

| O | B | A | F | G | K | M |

BRIGHT STARS NORTH CIRCLE COLOUR MAP

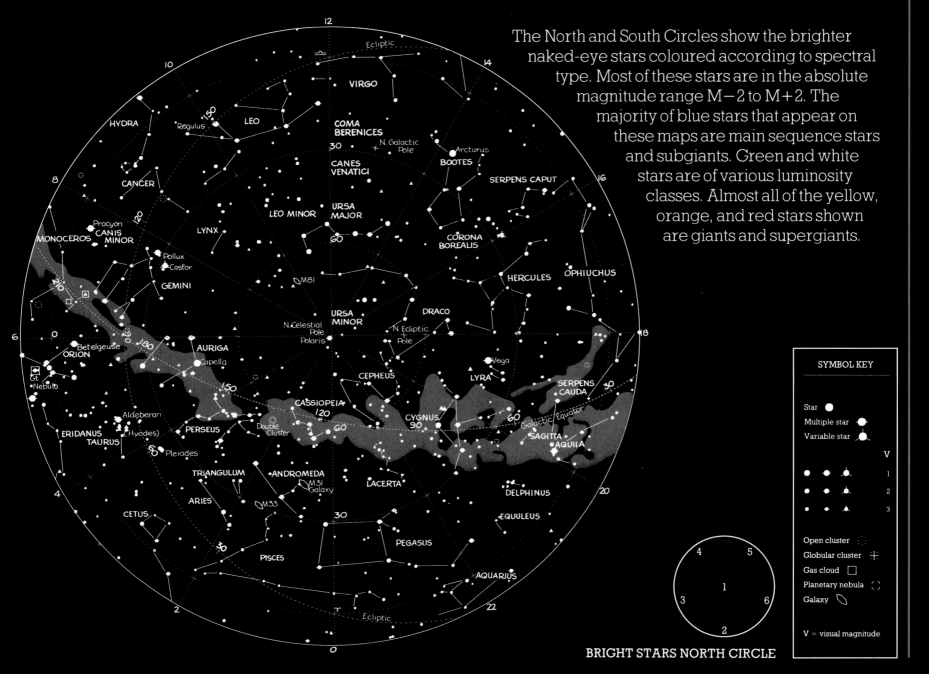

The North and South Circles show the brighter naked-eye stars coloured according to spectral type. Most of these stars are in the absolute magnitude range M−2 to M+2. The majority of blue stars that appear on these maps are main sequence stars and subgiants. Green and white stars are of various luminosity classes. Almost all of the yellow, orange, and red stars shown are giants and supergiants.

SYMBOL KEY

Star	●
Multiple star	●–
Variable star	●⭒

			V
●	●	⭒	1
●	●	⭒	2
●	•	⭒	3

Open cluster	⋮⋮
Globular cluster	⊕
Gas cloud	☐
Planetary nebula	⟨⟩
Galaxy	◳

V = visual magnitude

BRIGHT STARS NORTH CIRCLE

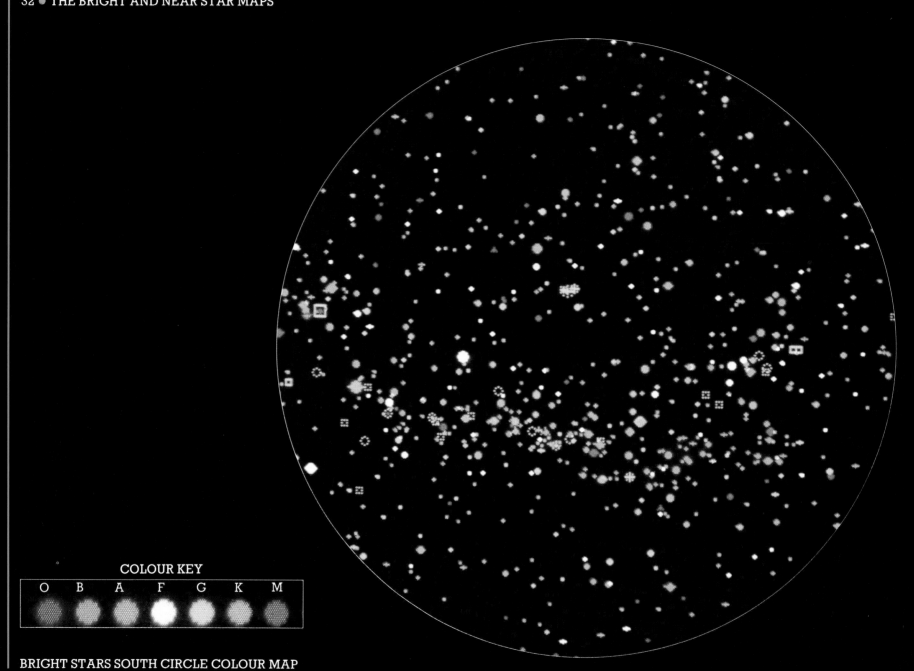

COLOUR KEY

O   B   A   F   G   K   M

BRIGHT STARS SOUTH CIRCLE COLOUR MAP

Ecliptic

CETUS

AQUARIUS

330

South
Galactic
Pole

SCULPTOR

PISCIS
AUSTRINUS

CAPRICORNUS

20

ERIDANUS

PHOENIX

GRUS

300

Achernar 60 TUCANA

INDUS

HOROLOGIUM

Small
Magellanic
Cloud

CORONA AUS.

Galactic Equator

SERPENS
CAUDA

RETICULUM

CAELUM

DORADO

HYDRUS

PAVO

TELESCOPIUM

30

SAGITTARIUS

LEPUS

Great
Nebula

ORION

COLUMBA

Large
Magellanic
Cloud

S.Celestial

OCTANS

18

30

S.Ecliptic
Pole

CHAMAELEON

PICTOR

Canopus

VOLANS

APUS

ARA

SCORPIUS

OPHIUCHUS

PUPPIS

TRIANGULUM
AUS.

Sirius

210

CANIS
MAJOR

CARINA

MUSCA CIRCINUS

330

Rigel Centurus

Antares

SERPENS
CAPUT

MONOCEROS

240

PUPPIS

270

VELA

CRUX

300

Agena

CENTAURUS

LIBRA

16

CANIS MINOR

PYXIS

Procyon

ANTLIA

HYDRA

CORVUS

240

Spica

VIRGO

210

Ecliptic

10

14

12

7   11

8   10

12

9

SYMBOL KEY

Star ●

Multiple star ●

Variable star ●

V

● ● ▲   1

● ● ▲   2

● ● ▲   3

Open cluster ⣿

Globular cluster ✛

Gas cloud ☐

Planetary nebula ⟨ ⟩

Galaxy ⬡

V = visual magnitude

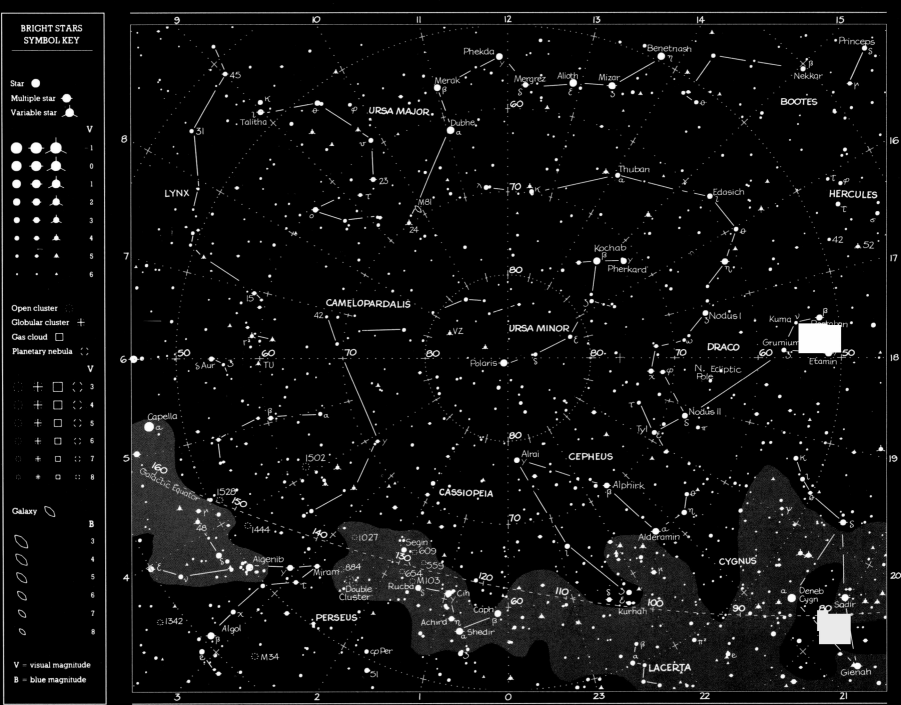

3-D DEPTH KEY

pc

1.0

2.0

3.0

4.0

plane
of   5.0
page

6.0

7.0

8.0

9.0

10.0

12.0

15.0

20.0

25.0

50.0

100.0

250.0

500.0

1.0K

2.5K

5.0K

10.0K

50.0K

500.0K

pc = distance in parsecs

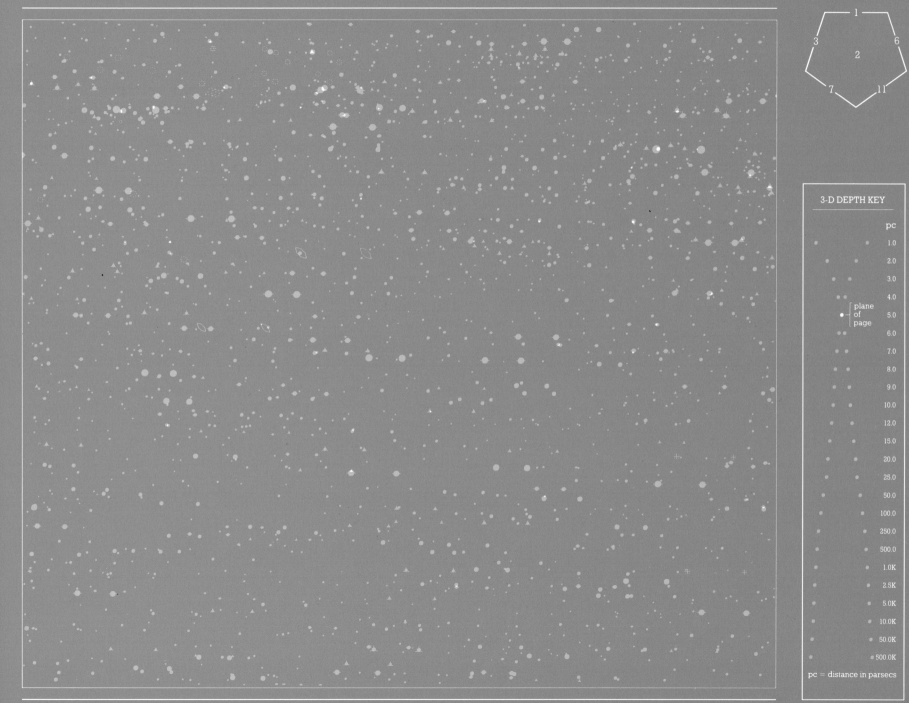

3-D DEPTH KEY

pc

1.0

2.0

3.0

4.0

plane
of
page   5.0

6.0

7.0

8.0

9.0

10.0

12.0

15.0

20.0

25.0

50.0

100.0

250.0

500.0

1.0K

2.5K

5.0K

10.0K

50.0K

500.0K

pc = distance in parsecs

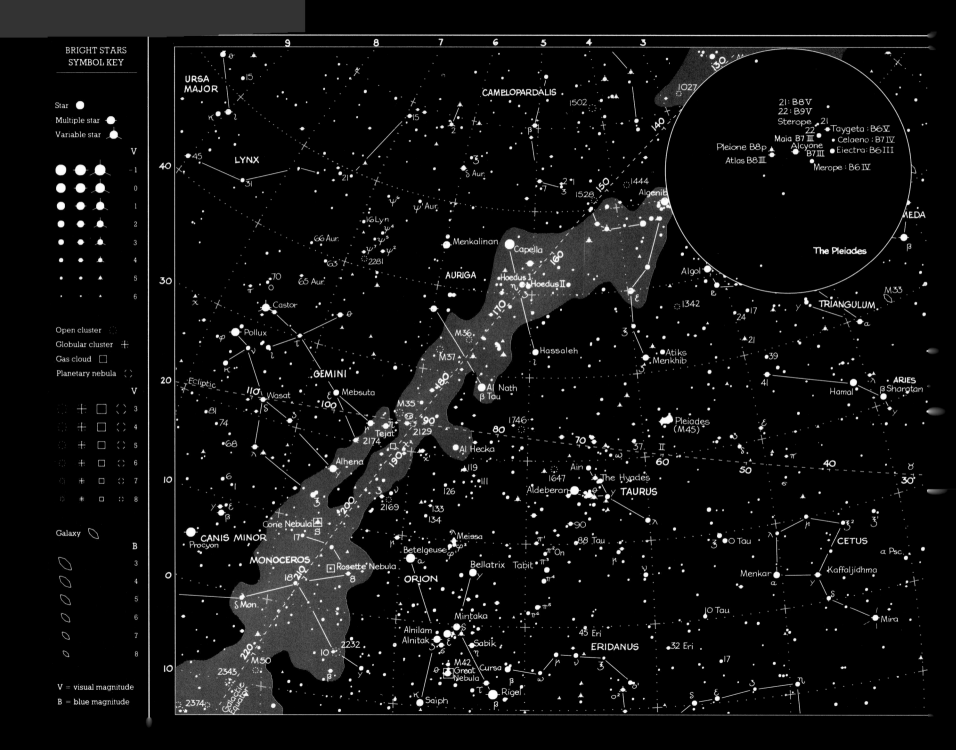

**BRIGHT STARS
SYMBOL KEY**

Star ●
Multiple star ◉
Variable star ◐

V
-1
0
1
2
3
4
5
6

Open cluster
Globular cluster
Gas cloud
Planetary nebula

V
3
4
5
6
7
8

Galaxy

B
3
4
5
6
7
8

V = visual magnitude

B = blue magnitude

URSA
MAJOR

15

CAMELOPARDALIS

1502

1027

45
LYNX

31

21

40

16 Lyn

66 Aur

63

2281

70
65 Aur

Castor

Pollux

GEMINI

Mebsuta

Wasat
110

100

81

74

68

Tejat
2174

M35

2129

Alhena

6

CANIS MINOR
Procyon

MONOCEROS

17

Cone Nebula
S

18

S Mon

2232

2343
M50

2374

Galactic Equator

10

ORION

Rosette Nebula
8

Betelgeuse

Bellatrix Tabit

Meissa

Mintaka

Alnilam
Alnitak

Sabik

M42
Great
Nebula

Saiph

Rigel

Cursa

45 Eri

ERIDANUS

32 Eri

17

Menkalinan

Capella

AURIGA

Hoedus I
Hoedus II

M36

Hassaleh

M37

Al Nath
β Tau

Al Hecka

119

111

126

133

134

90

1746

Pleiades
(M45)

The Hyades

Aldebaran

TAURUS

Ain

1647

88 Tau

On

10 Tau

O Tau

90

Algol

Algenib

1528 150

1444

1342

24 17

21

39

41

Hamal

1502

37.

70

60

50

40

30

II

130

140

160

170

180

190

200

220

210

The Pleiades

21: B8V
22: B9V
Sterope 21
22 Taygeta : B6V
Maia B7 III Celaeno : B7 IV
Pleione B8p Alcyone Electra: B6 III
Atlas B8 III B7 III

Merope : B6 IV

...EDA

β

M33

TRIANGULUM

α

ARIES
β Sharatan

γ

CETUS

α Psc

Menkar
α

Kaffaljidhma

γ

δ

Mira

Atiks
Menkhib

Ecliptic

3-D DEPTH KEY

pc

1.0

2.0

3.0

4.0

plane
of   5.0
page

6.0

7.0

8.0

9.0

10.0

12.0

15.0

20.0

25.0

50.0

100.0

250.0

500.0

1.0K

2.5K

5.0K

10.0K

50.0K

500.0K

pc = distance in parsecs

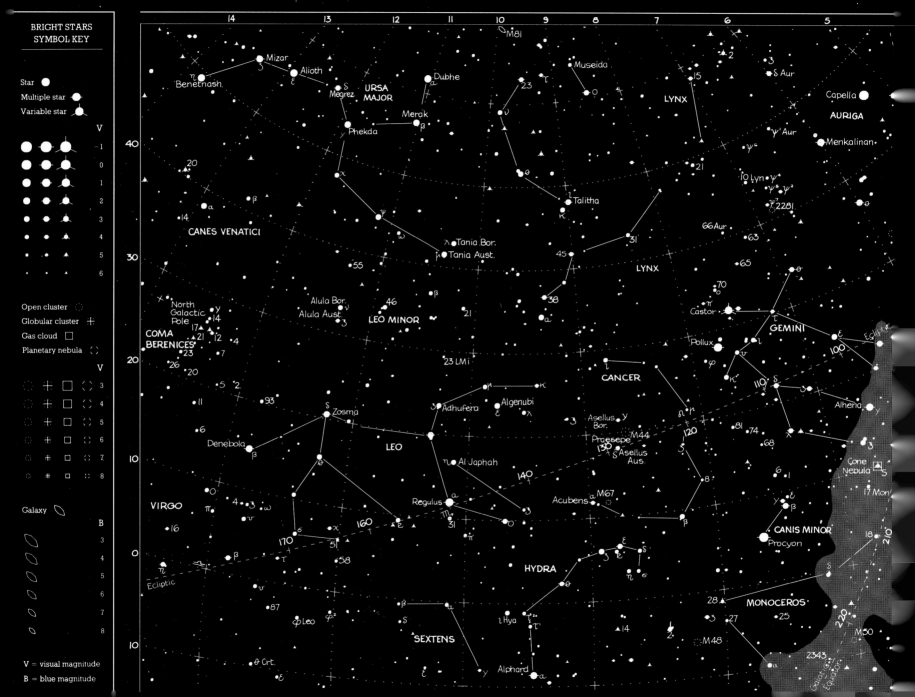

BRIGHT STARS
SYMBOL KEY

Star ●
Multiple star
Variable star

V
−1
0
1
2
3
4
5
6

Open cluster
Globular cluster
Gas cloud
Planetary nebula

V
3
4
5
6
7
8

Galaxy

B
3
4
5
6
7
8

V = visual magnitude

B = blue magnitude

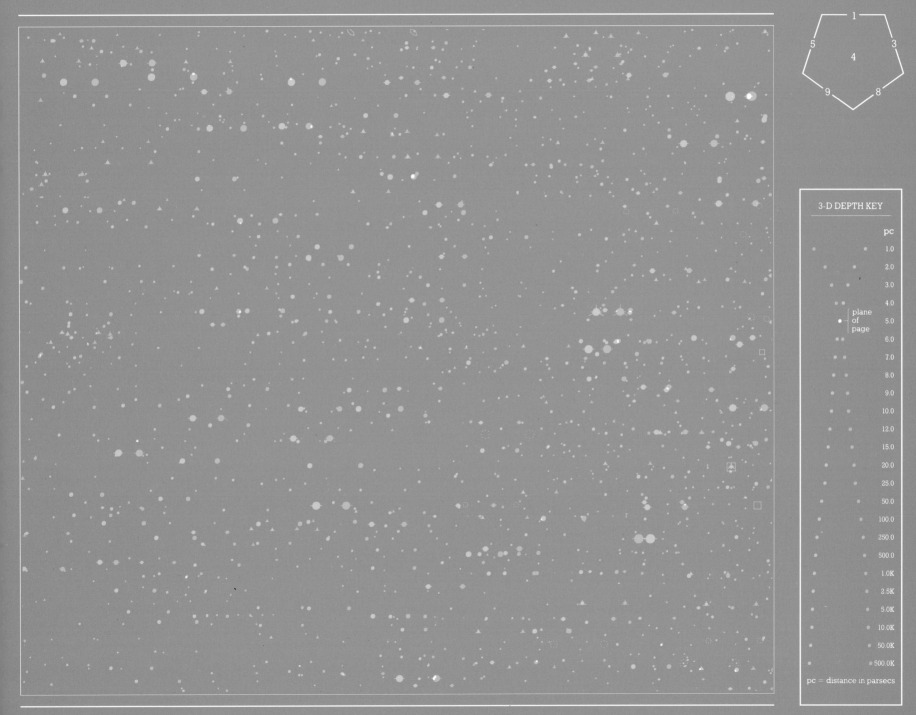

3-D DEPTH KEY

pc

1.0
2.0
3.0
4.0
plane of page ● 5.0
6.0
7.0
8.0
9.0
10.0
12.0
15.0
20.0
25.0
50.0
100.0
250.0
500.0
1.0K
2.5K
5.0K
10.0K
50.0K
500.0K

pc = distance in parsecs

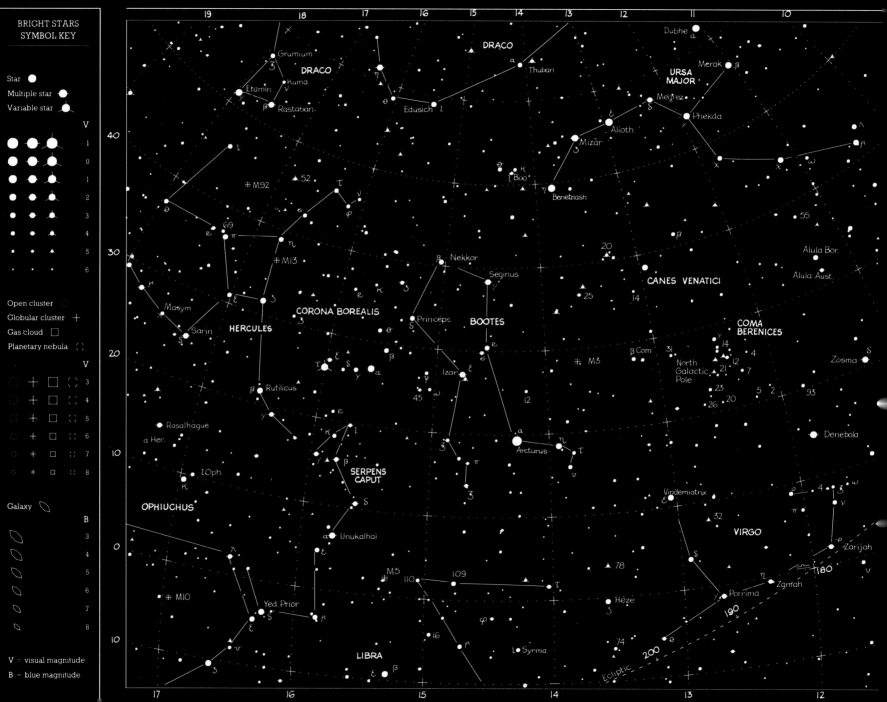

**BRIGHT STARS
SYMBOL KEY**

Star ●
Multiple star ●
Variable star ●

V
−1
0
1
2
3
4
5
6

Open cluster
Globular cluster +
Gas cloud □
Planetary nebula

V
3
4
5
6
7
8

Galaxy

B
3
4
5
6
7
8

V = visual magnitude

B = blue magnitude

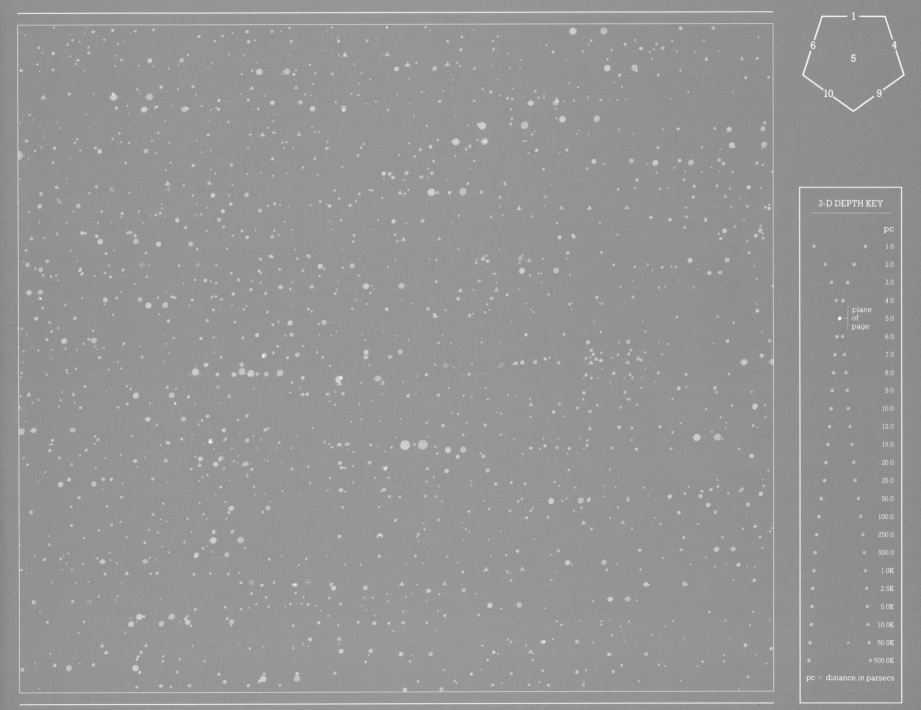

3-D DEPTH KEY

pc

1.0

2.0

3.0

4.0

plane
of
page   5.0

6.0

7.0

8.0

9.0

10.0

12.0

15.0

20.0

25.0

50.0

100.0

250.0

500.0

1.0K

2.5K

5.0K

10.0K

50.0K

500.0K

pc = distance in parsecs

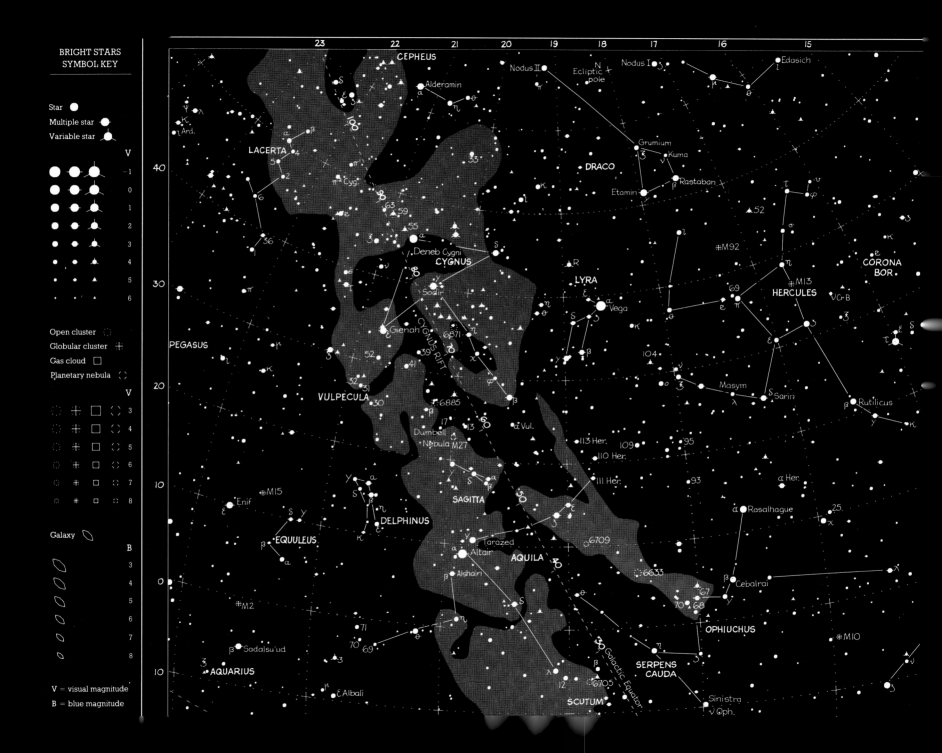

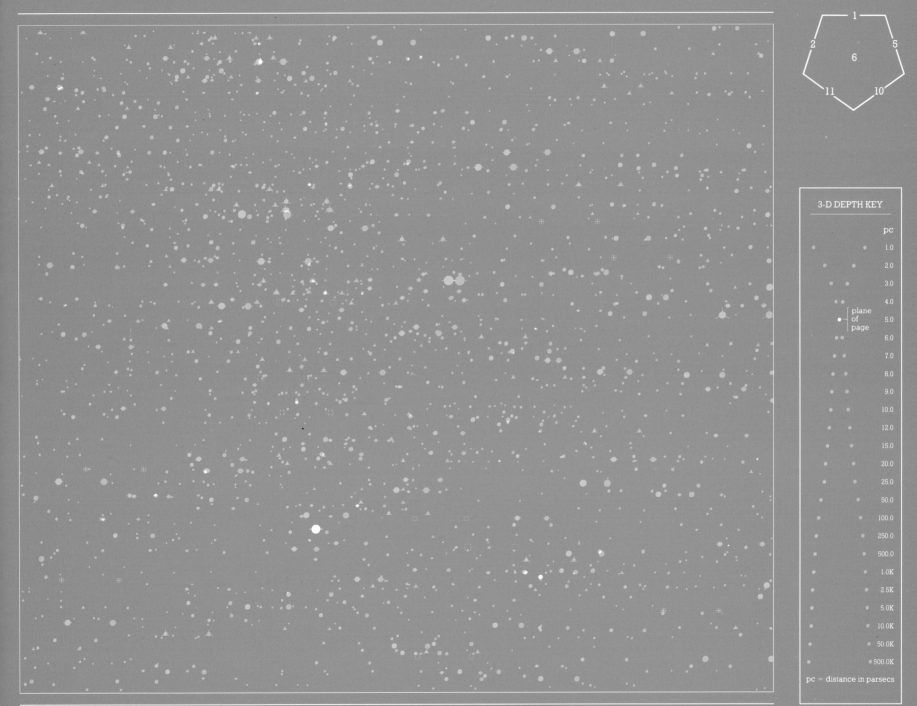

pc

1.0

2.0

3.0

4.0

plane
of
page 5.0

6.0

7.0

8.0

9.0

10.0

12.0

15.0

20.0

25.0

50.0

100.0

250.0

500.0

1.0K

2.5K

5.0K

10.0K

50.0K

500.0K

pc = distance in parsecs

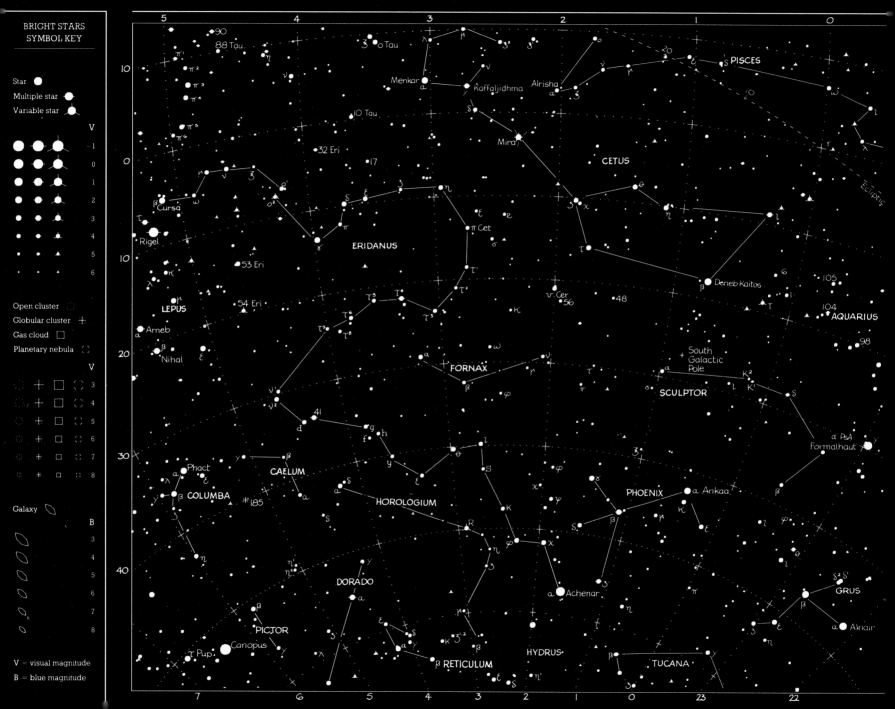

3   2

7

8   11

12

3-D DEPTH KEY

pc

1.0

2.0

3.0

4.0

plane
of   5.0
page

6.0

7.0

8.0

9.0

10.0

12.0

15.0

20.0

25.0

50.0

100.0

250.0

500.0

1.0K

2.5K

5.0K

10.0K

50.0K

500.0K

pc = distance in parsecs

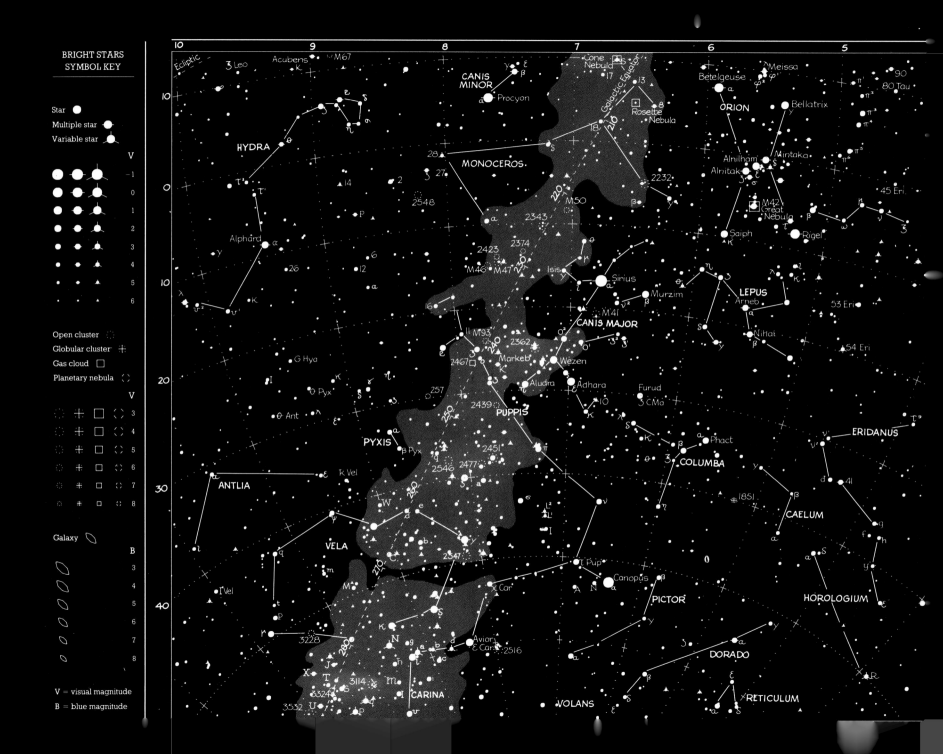

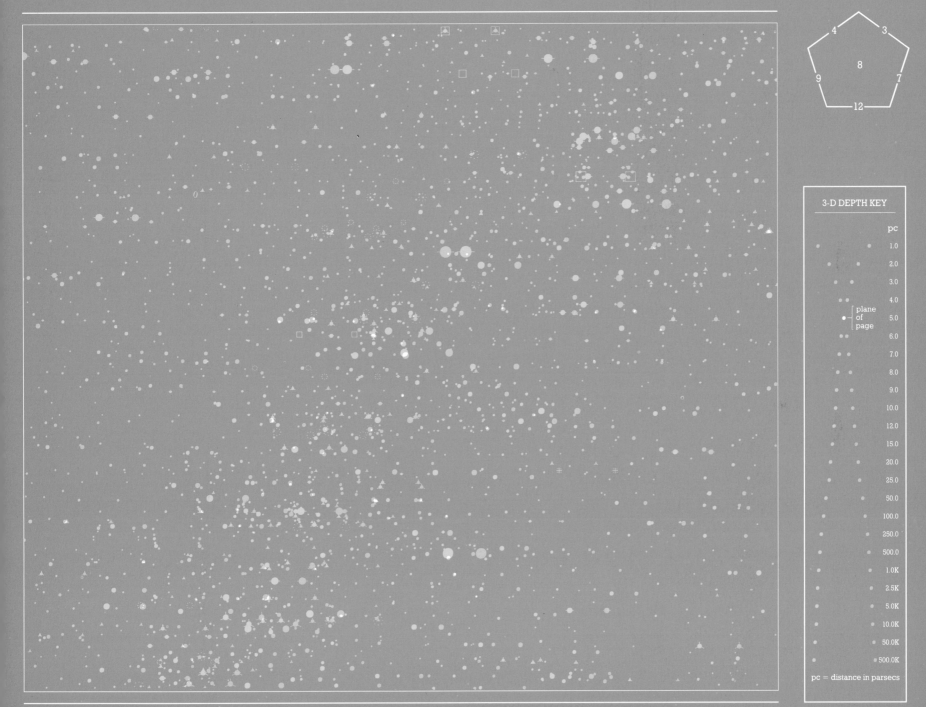

4 3
8
9 7
12

3-D DEPTH KEY

pc

1.0

2.0

3.0

4.0

plane
of   5.0
page

6.0

7.0

8.0

9.0

10.0

12.0

15.0

20.0

25.0

50.0

100.0

250.0

500.0

1.0K

2.5K

5.0K

10.0K

50.0K

500.0K

pc = distance in parsecs

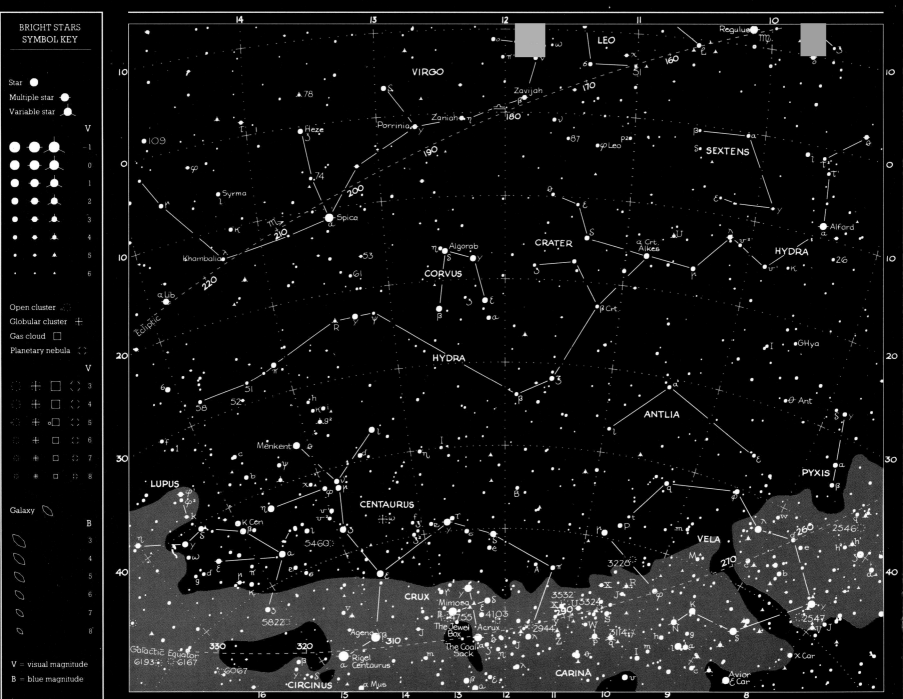

5 4

9

10 8

12

3-D DEPTH KEY

pc

1.0

2.0

3.0

4.0

plane
of   5.0
page

6.0

7.0

8.0

9.0

10.0

12.0

15.0

20.0

25.0

50.0

100.0

250.0

500.0

1.0K

2.5K

5.0K

10.0K

50.0K

500.0K

pc = distance in parsecs

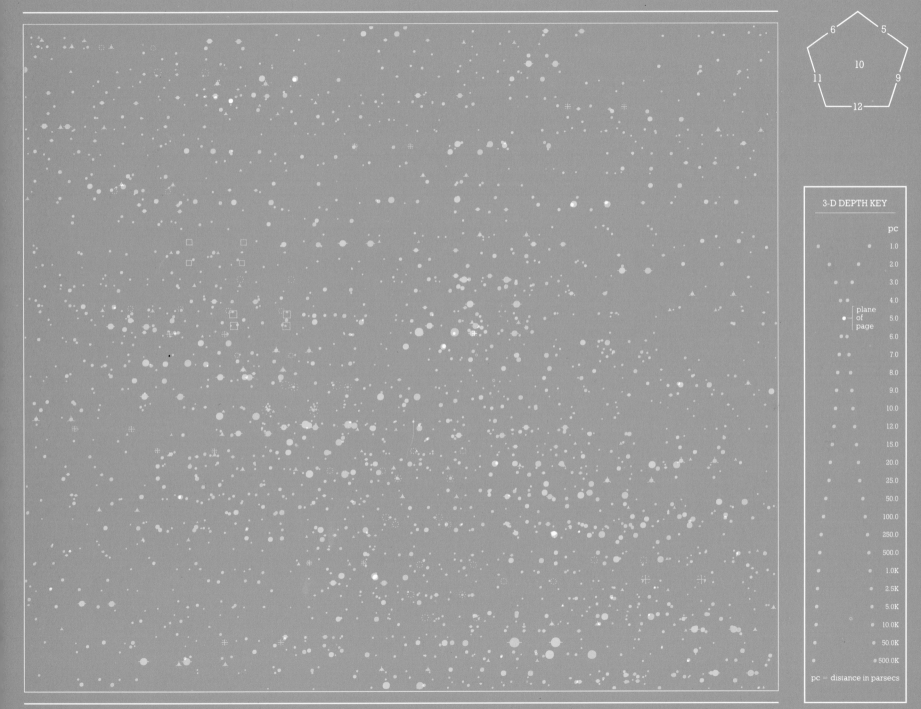

6   5

10

11   9

12

3-D DEPTH KEY

pc

1.0

2.0

3.0

4.0

plane
of   5.0
page

6.0

7.0

8.0

9.0

10.0

12.0

15.0

20.0

25.0

50.0

100.0

250.0

500.0

1.0K

2.5K

5.0K

10.0K

50.0K

500.0K

pc = distance in parsecs

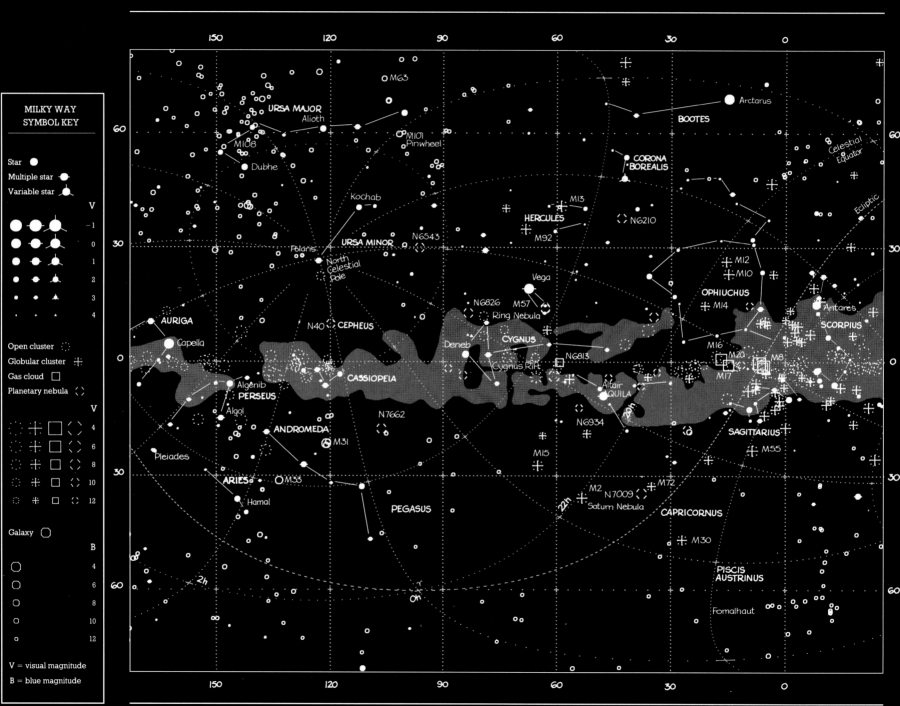

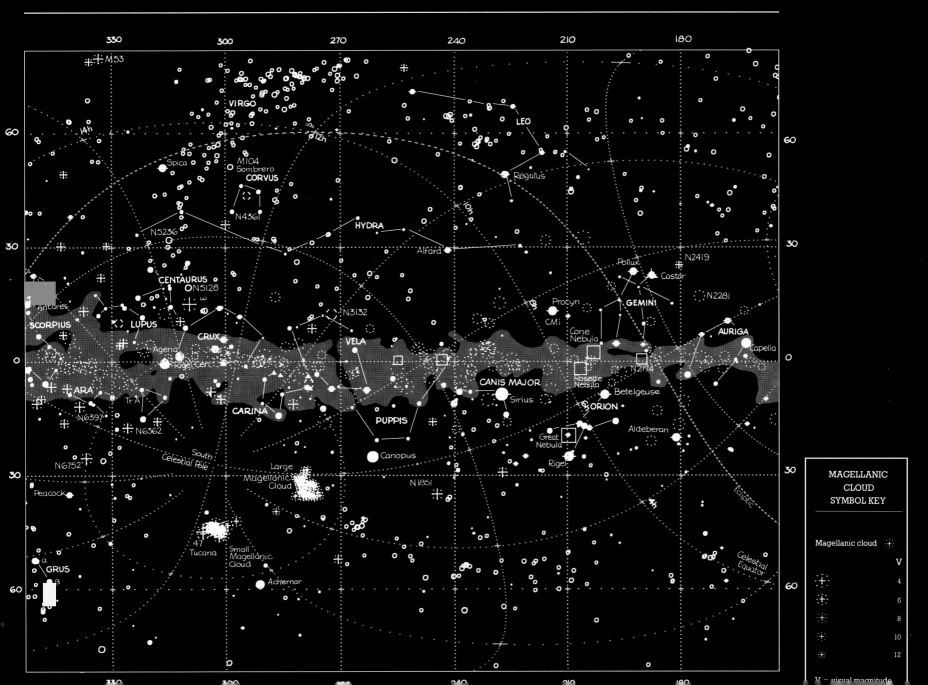

330   300   270   240   210   180

60   60

M53

14h

VIRGO

Spica

M104
Sombrero

CORVUS

N4361

N5236

HYDRA

LEO

Regulus

Alfard

N2419

30   30

CENTAURUS
N5128
ω

Pollux
Castor

N2281

Antares

SCORPIUS

LUPUS

CRUX

VELA

Agena

Rigel Cen

Procyn

CMi

Cone
Nebula

GEMINI

AURIGA

Capella

0   0

ARA

Tr A

CARINA

PUPPIS

CANIS MAJOR

Sirius

Rosette
Nebula

Betelgeuse

ORION

N2174

Aldeberan

N6397

N6362

South
Celestial Pole

Canopus

Great
Nebula

Rigel

30   30

N6752

Peacock

Large
Magellanic
Cloud

N1851

Ecliptic

47
Tucana

Small
Magellanic
Cloud

Celestial
Equator

GRUS

α

β

Achernar

60   60

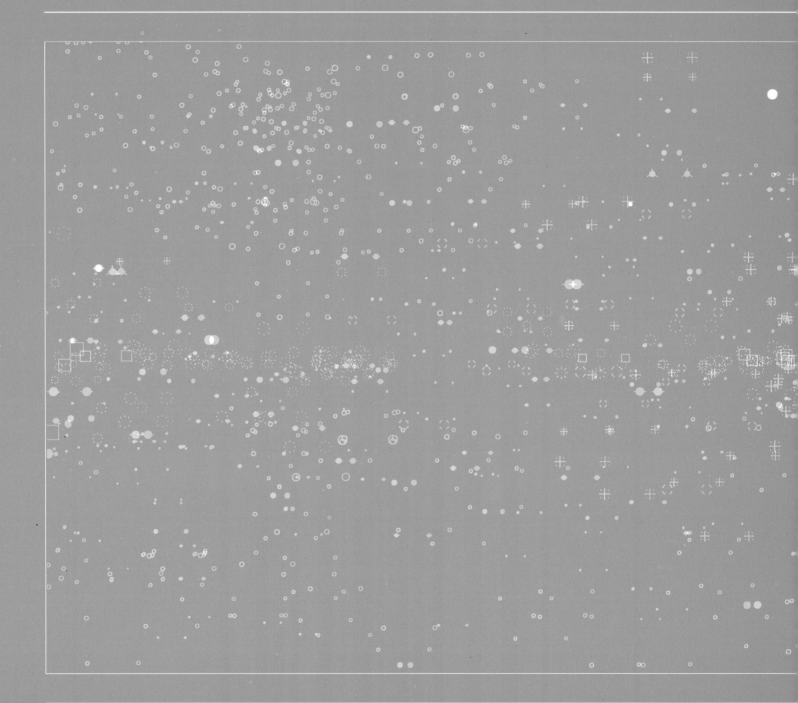

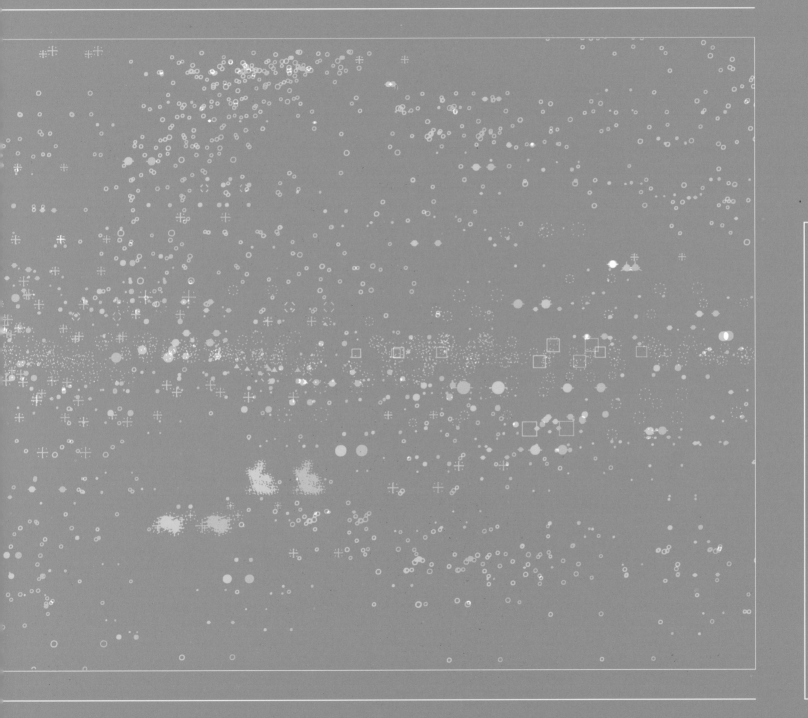

3-D DEPTH KEY

pc

3.0

4.0

5.0

6.0

7.0

8.0

9.0

plane
of   10.0
page

12.0

15.0

20.0

25.0

50.0

100.0

250.0

500.0

1.0K

2.5K

5.0K

10.0K

50.0K

500.0K

pc = distance in parsecs

3-D DEPTH KEY

	pc
	1.0
	2.0
	3.0
	4.0
plane of page	5.0
	6.0
	7.0
	8.0
	9.0
	10.0
	12.0
	15.0
	20.0
	25.0
	50.0
	100.0
	250.0
	500.0
	1.0K
	2.5K
	5.0K
	10.0K
	50.0K
	500.0K

pc = distance in parsecs

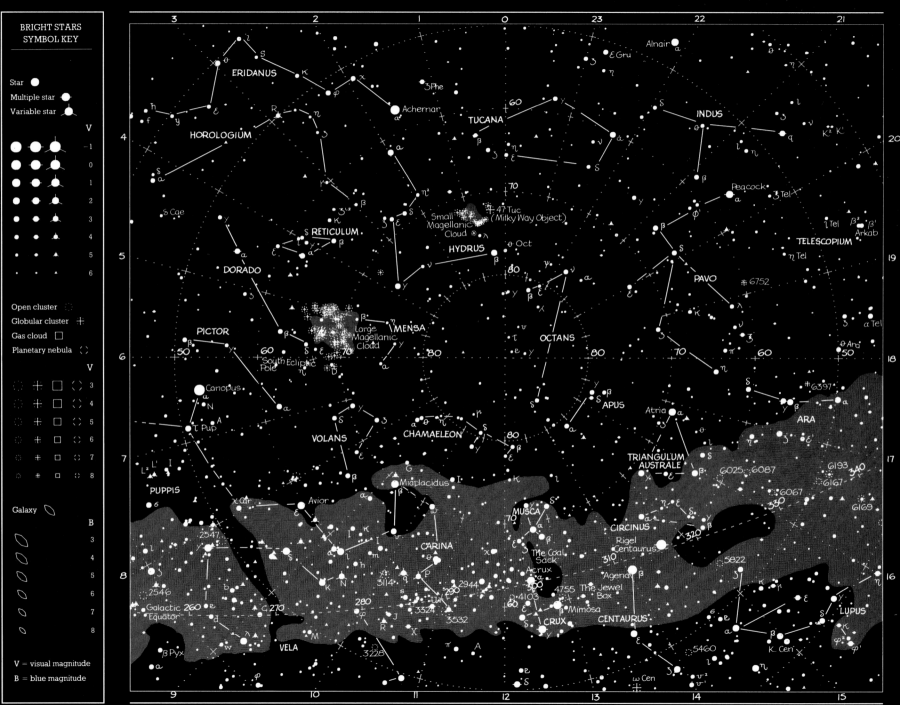

7 11
12
8 10
9

3-D DEPTH KEY

pc

1.0

2.0

3.0

4.0

plane
of 5.0
page

6.0

7.0

8.0

9.0

10.0

12.0

15.0

20.0

25.0

50.0

100.0

250.0

500.0

1.0K

2.5K

5.0K

10.0K

50.0K

500.0K

pc = distance in parsecs

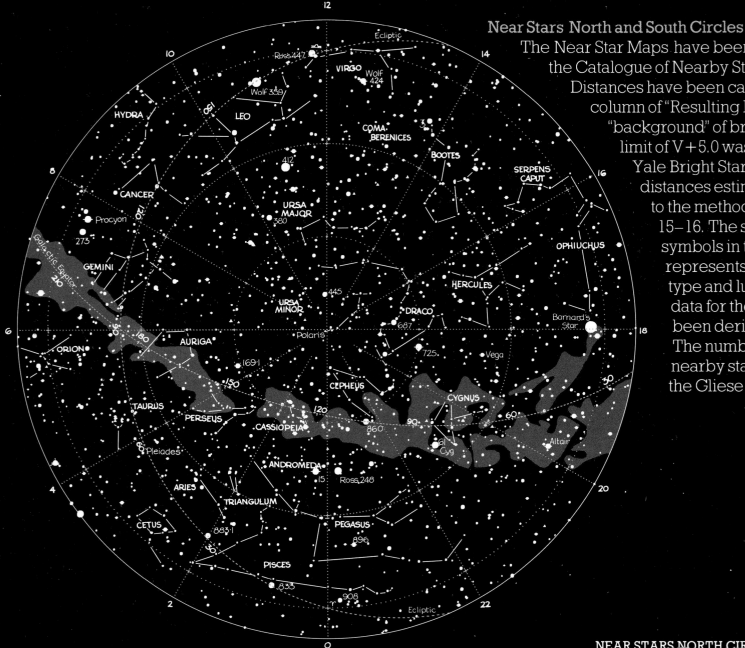

Near Stars North and South Circles

The Near Star Maps have been generated from the Catalogue of Nearby Stars (W. Gliese). Distances have been calculated from the column of "Resulting Parallax". A "background" of bright stars to a limit of V+5.0 was added from the Yale Bright Star Catalogue and distances estimated according to the method outlined on pages 15–16. The size of the star symbols in these maps represents distance. Spectral type and luminosity class data for the nearest stars has been derived from Gliese. The numbering of the nearby stars is according to the Gliese Catalogue.

NEAR STARS NORTH CIRCLE

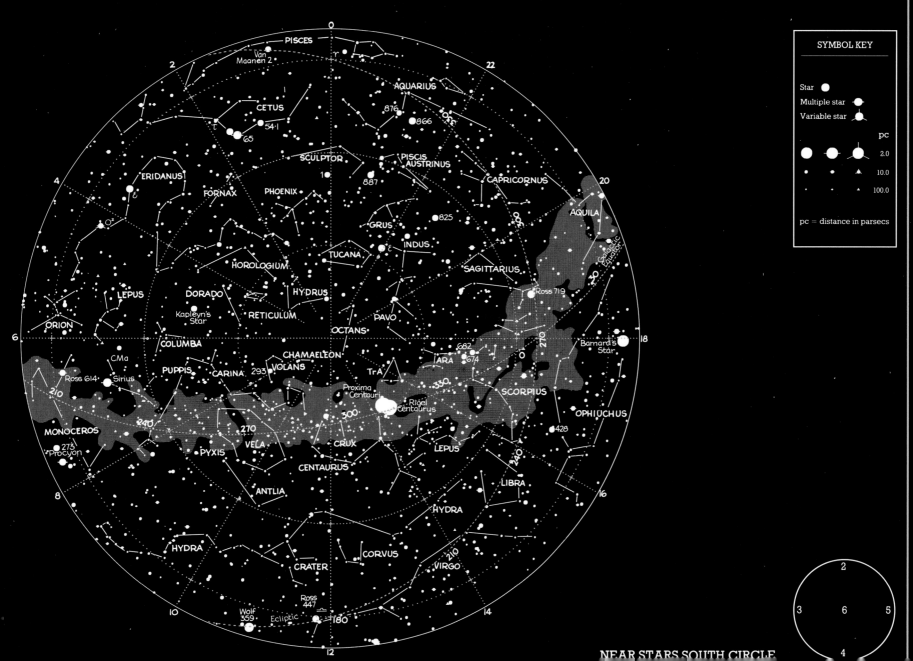

SYMBOL KEY

Star ●
Multiple star ●–
Variable star ☆

pc

2.0
10.0
100.0

pc = distance in parsecs

PISCES
Van Maanen 2
AQUARIUS
876
866
CETUS
54·1
65
SCULPTOR
PISCIS AUSTRINUS
887
ERIDANUS
ε
FORNAX
PHOENIX
CAPRICORNUS
20
AQUILA
825
GRUS
O²
INDUS
SAGITTARIUS
Galactic Equator
LEPUS
HOROLOGIUM
TUCANA
ORION
DORADO
HYDRUS
Kapteyn's Star
RETICULUM
PAVO
Ross 719
OCTANS
COLUMBA
Barnard's Star
6
CHAMAELEON
18
CMa
682
Ross 614
Sirius
VOLANS
ARA
674
PUPPIS
293
CARINA
TrA
Proxima Centauri
330
SCORPIUS
OPHIUCHUS
210
240
300
Rigel Centaurus
428
270
MONOCEROS
273
Procyon
PYXIS
VELA
CRUX
LEPUS
CENTAURUS
240
ANTLIA
LIBRA
8
HYDRA
HYDRA
CORVUS
210
CRATER
VIRGO
Ross 447
Wolf 359
Ecliptic
180
16
10
12
14

2
3   6   5
4

NEAR STARS SOUTH CIRCLE

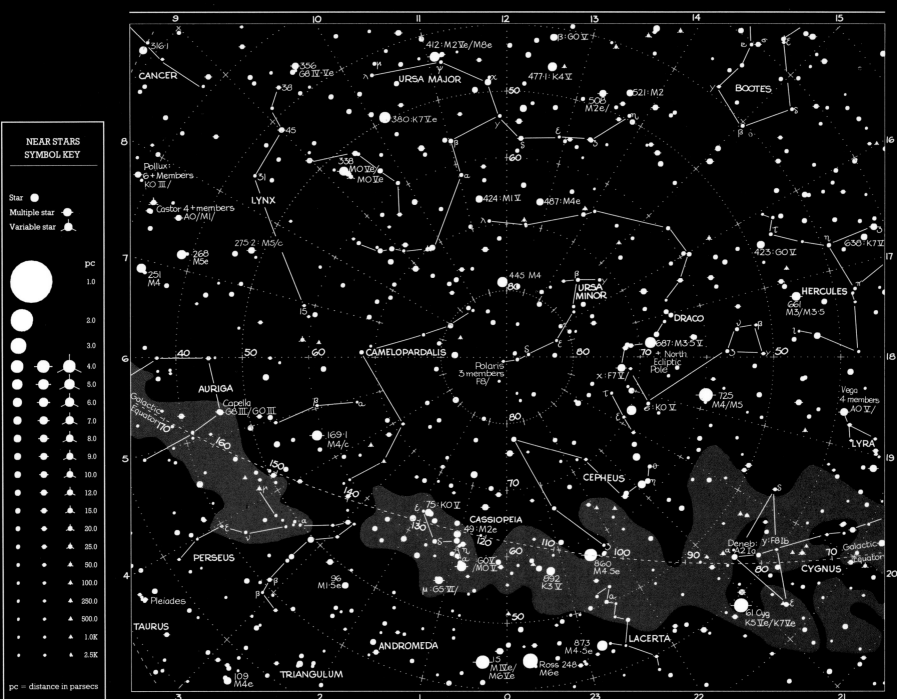

NEAR STARS
SYMBOL KEY

Star ●

Multiple star

Variable star

pc = distance in parsecs

pc
1.0
2.0
3.0
4.0
5.0
6.0
7.0
8.0
9.0
10.0
12.0
15.0
20.0
25.0
50.0
100.0
250.0
500.0
1.0K
2.5K

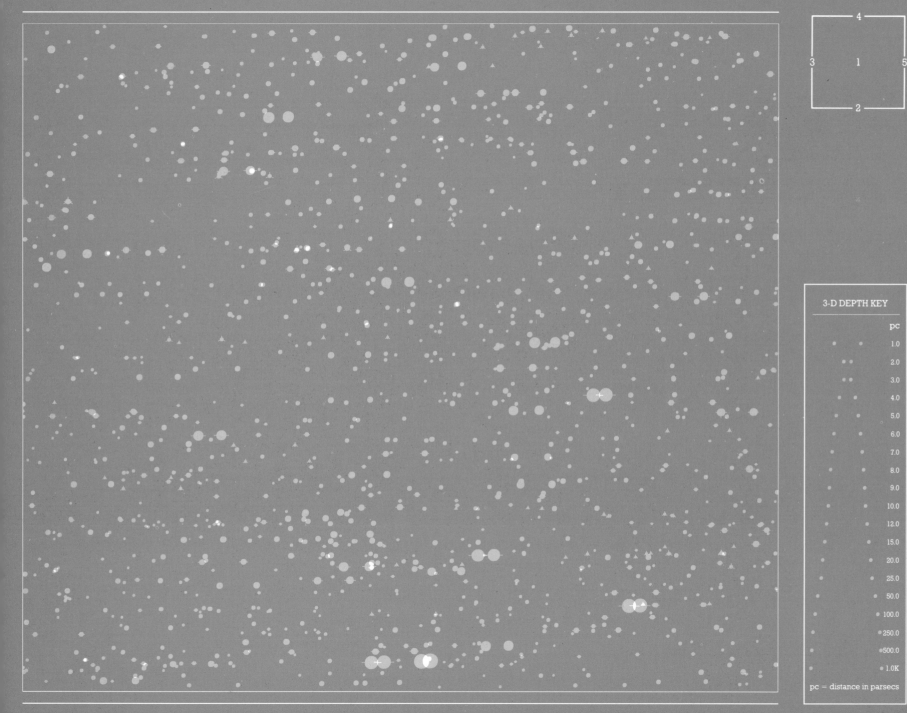

3-D DEPTH KEY

pc

1.0

2.0

3.0

4.0

5.0

6.0

7.0

8.0

9.0

10.0

12.0

15.0

20.0

25.0

50.0

100.0

250.0

500.0

1.0K

pc = distance in parsecs

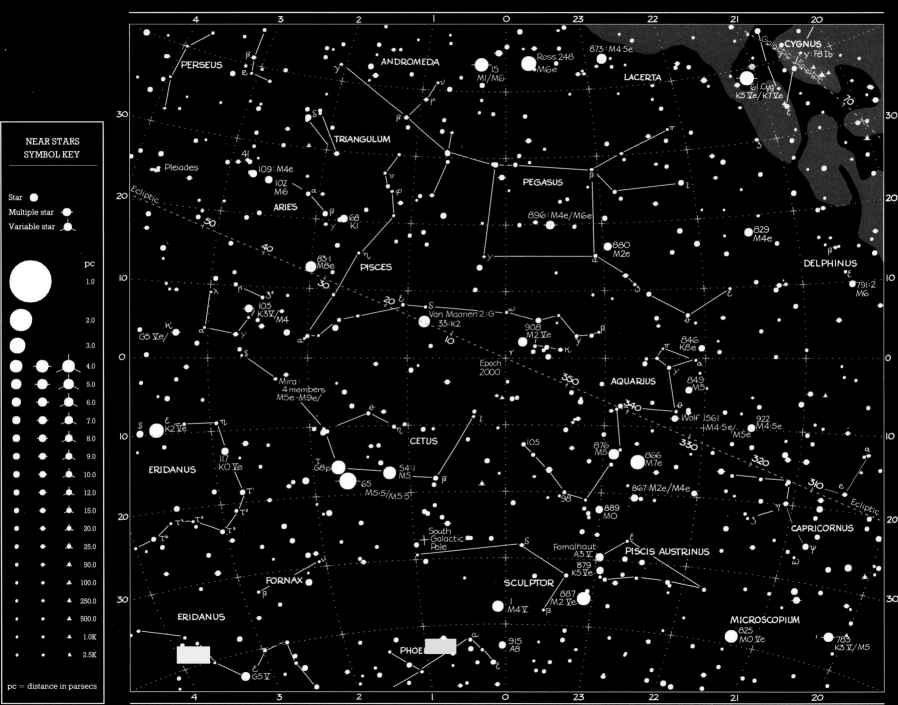

NEAR STARS
SYMBOL KEY

Star ●

Multiple star

Variable star

pc

1.0

2.0

3.0

4.0

5.0

6.0

7.0

8.0

9.0

10.0

12.0

15.0

20.0

25.0

50.0

100.0

250.0

500.0

1.0K

2.5K

pc = distance in parsecs

PERSEUS

β

e

ANDROMEDA

γ

ν

η

β

15
M1/M6

Ross 248
M6e

873 : M4·5e

LACERTA

CYGNUS

Galactic Equator

γ : F8 Ib

61 Cyg
K5 Ve/K7 Ve

ε

70

δ

TRIANGULUM

β

ι

PEGASUS

β

ι

DELPHINUS

β

ε

41

109 : M4e

102
M6

α

β

γ

68
K1

υ

φ

ARIES

896 : M4e/M6e

829
M4e

791 : 2
M6

Pleiades

Ecliptic

50

40

30

83·1
M8e

η

PISCES

τ

880
M2e

α

δ

908
M2 Ve

λ

η

3²

105
K3 V/
M4

ι

20

δ

Van Maanen 2 : G
33 : K2

ω

γ

β

846
K8e

849
M5

κ

α

γ

α

10

γ

846
K8e

G5 Ve/

κ

α

γ

δ

Epoch
2000

350

AQUARIUS

θ

π

α

Mira :
4 members
M5e-M9e/

θ

η

ι

340

Wolf 1561
M4·5e/

922
M4·5e

δ
K2 Ve

ε

η

CETUS

105

876
M5

866
M7e

330

320

ERIDANUS

117
KO Ve

τ
G8p

54 : 1
M5

β

98

867 : M2e/M4e

310

ε

Ecliptic

τ¹

65
M5·5/M5·5

889
MO

η

3

τ²

CAPRICORNUS

τ⁵ τ⁴

τ³

South
Galactic
Pole

S

Fomalhaut
A3 V

ε

PISCIS AUSTRINUS

ω

ψ

τ⁶

ν

FORNAX

β

879
K5 Ve

SCULPTOR

887
M2 Ve

β

MICROSCOPIUM

825
MO Ve

783
K3 V/M5

ERIDANUS

ε
G5 V

PHOE

α

ε

1
M4 V

915
A8

β

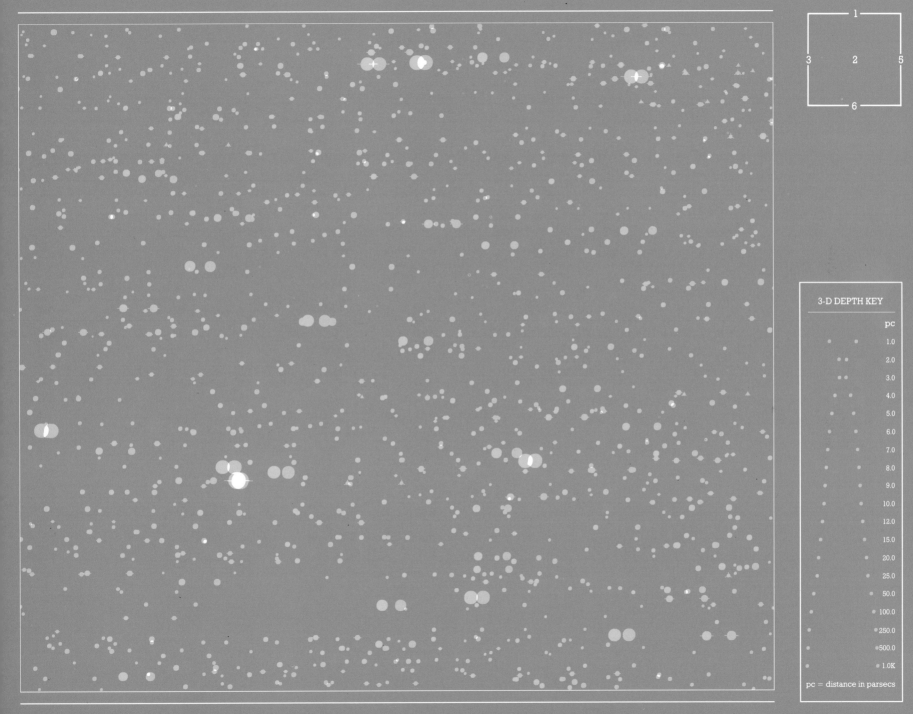

3-D DEPTH KEY

pc

1.0

2.0

3.0

4.0

5.0

6.0

7.0

8.0

9.0

10.0

12.0

15.0

20.0

25.0

50.0

100.0

250.0

500.0

1.0K

pc = distance in parsecs

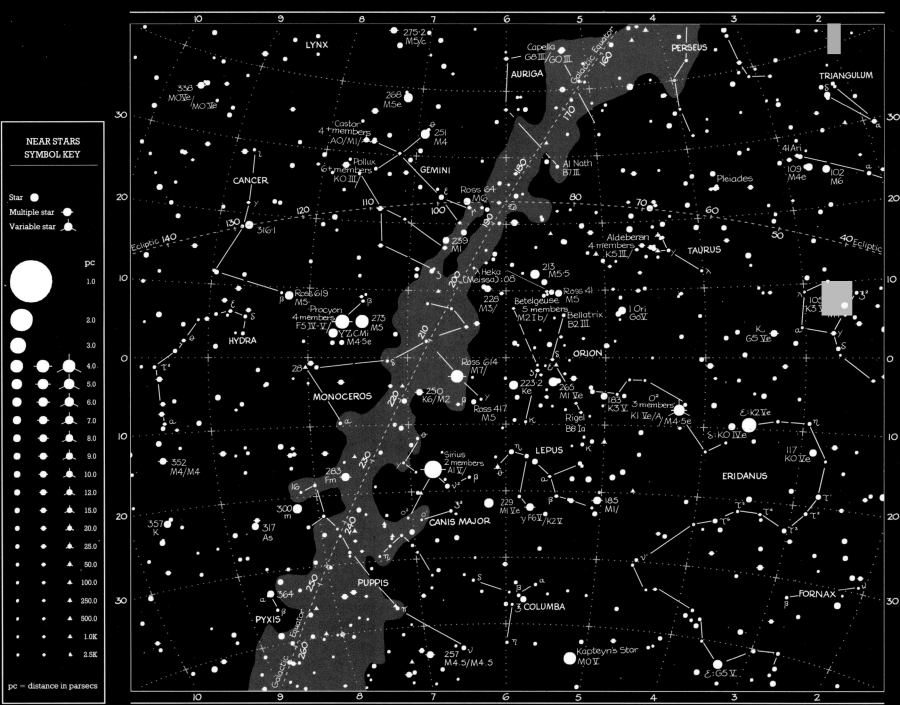

NEAR STARS
SYMBOL KEY

Star ●
Multiple star
Variable star

pc

1.0
2.0
3.0
4.0
5.0
6.0
7.0
8.0
9.0
10.0
12.0
15.0
20.0
25.0
50.0
100.0
250.0
500.0
1.0K
2.5K

pc = distance in parsecs

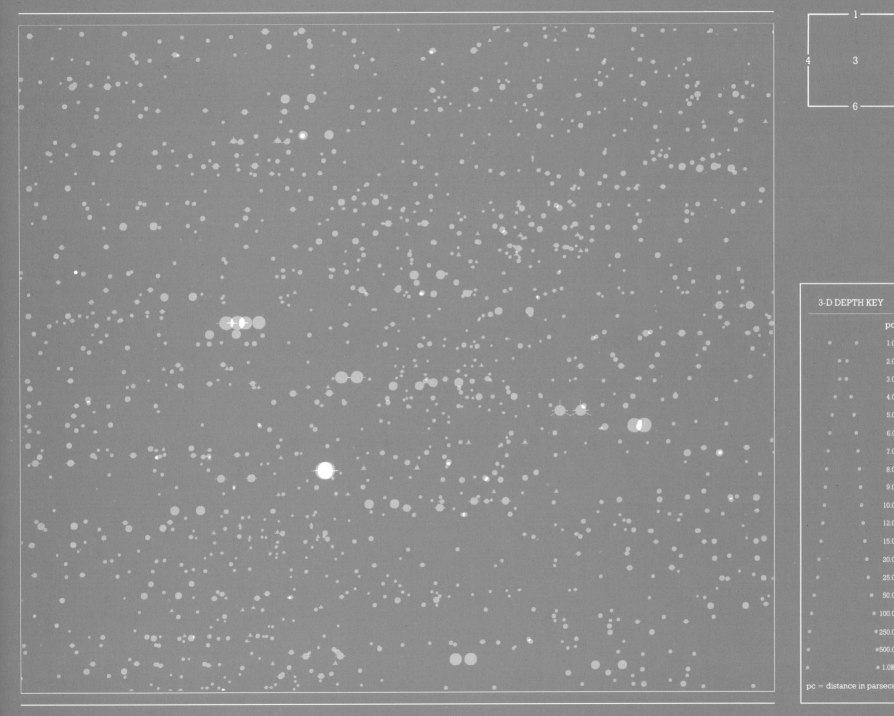

3-D DEPTH KEY

pc

1.0

2.0

3.0

4.0

5.0

6.0

7.0

8.0

9.0

10.0

12.0

15.0

20.0

25.0

50.0

100.0

250.0

500.0

1.0K

pc = distance in parsecs

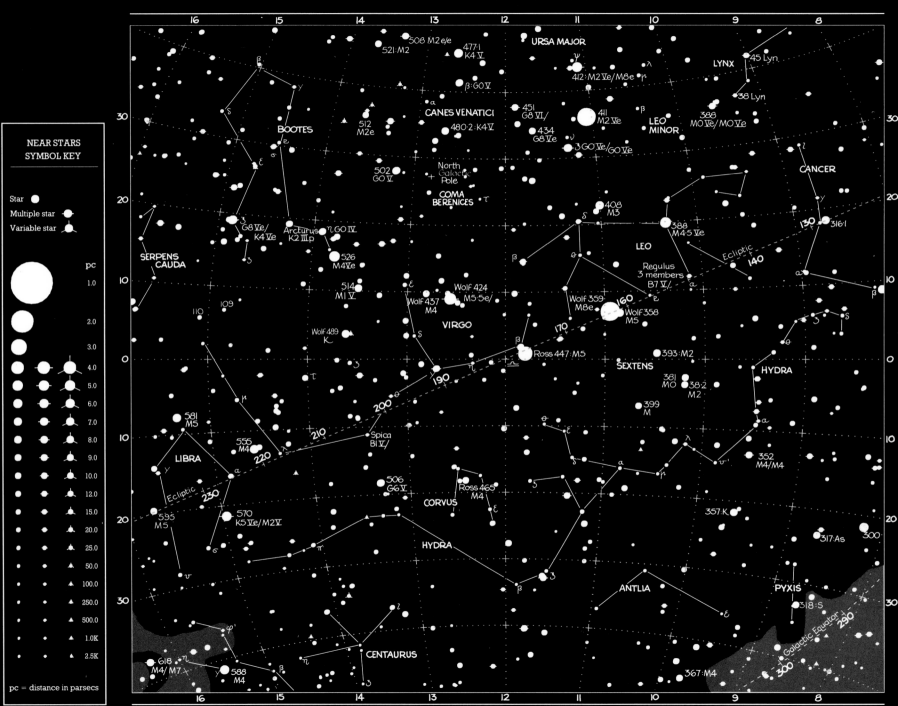

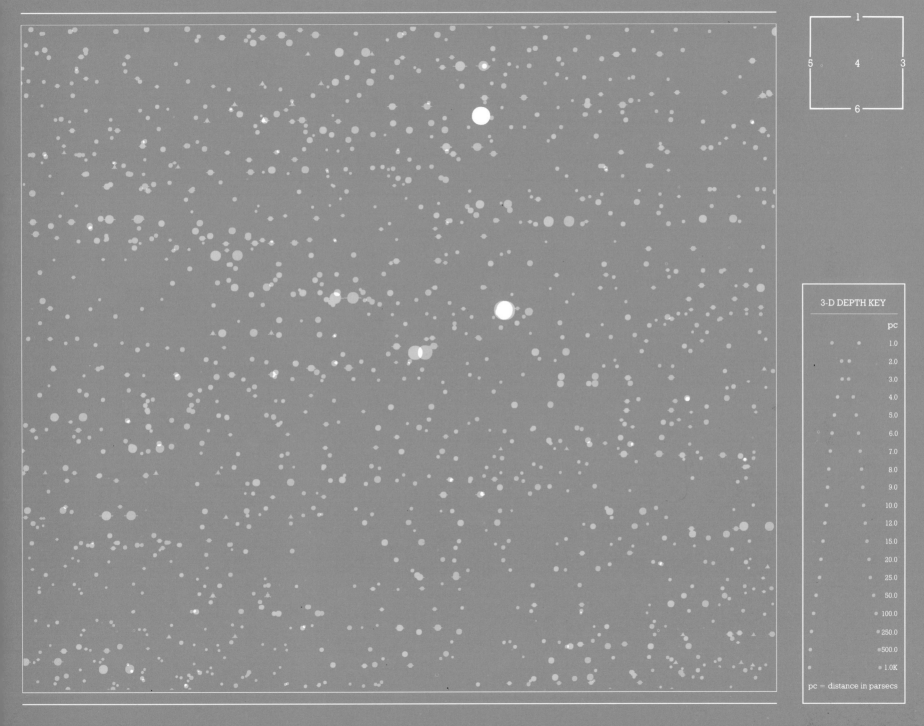

3-D DEPTH KEY

pc

		1.0
		2.0
		3.0
		4.0
		5.0
		6.0
		7.0
		8.0
		9.0
		10.0
		12.0
		15.0
		20.0
		25.0
		50.0
		100.0
		250.0
		500.0
		1.0K

pc = distance in parsecs

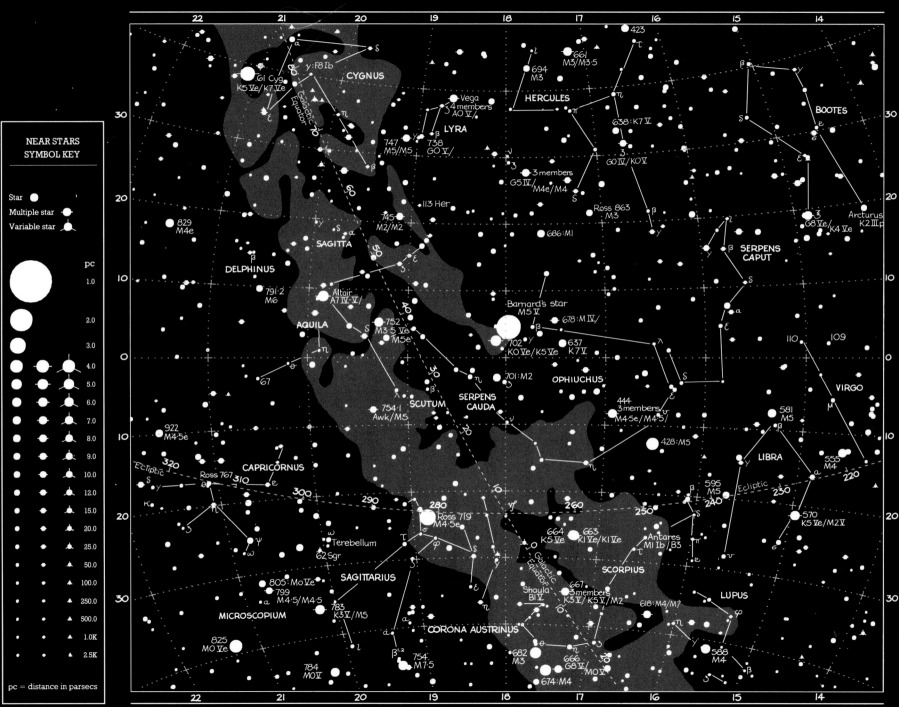

NEAR STARS
SYMBOL KEY

Star ●
Multiple star ◑
Variable star ◑

pc

1.0
2.0
3.0
4.0
5.0
6.0
7.0
8.0
9.0
10.0
12.0
15.0
20.0
25.0
50.0
100.0
250.0
500.0
1.0K
2.5K

pc = distance in parsecs

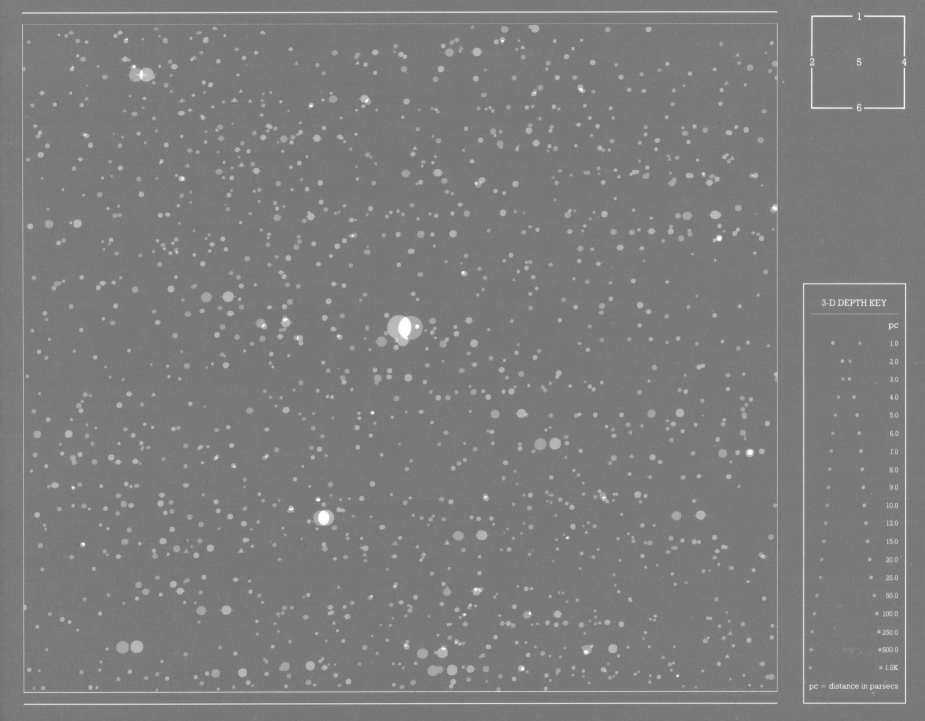

3-D DEPTH KEY

pc

1.0
2.0
3.0
4.0
5.0
6.0
7.0
8.0
9.0
10.0
12.0
15.0
20.0
25.0
50.0
100.0
250.0
500.0
1.0K

pc = distance in parsecs

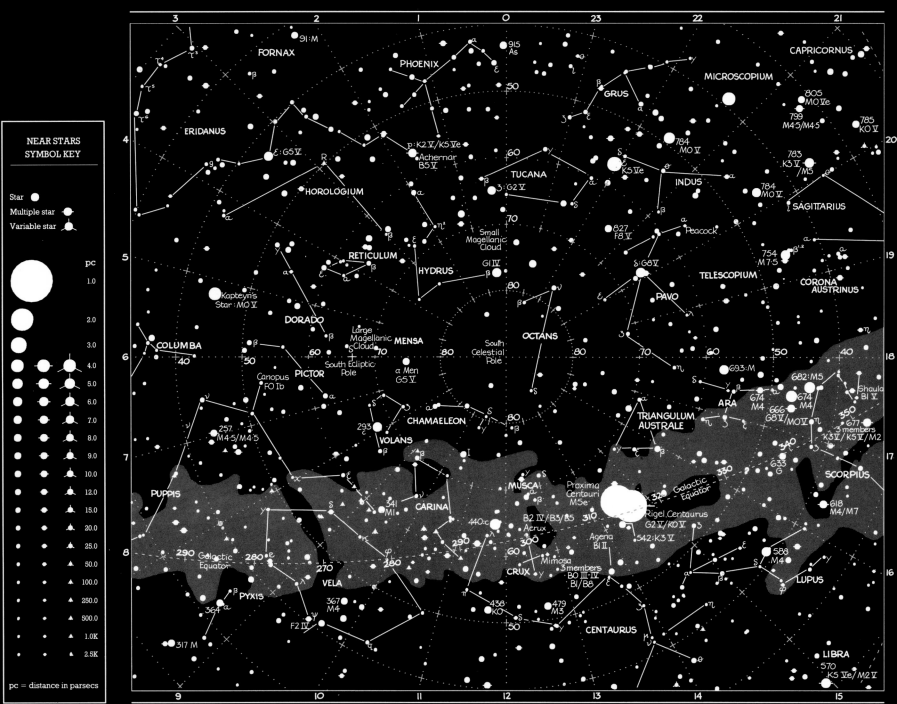

NEAR STARS SYMBOL KEY

Star ●

Multiple star

Variable star

	pc
	1.0
	2.0
	3.0
	4.0
	5.0
	6.0
	7.0
	8.0
	9.0
	10.0
	12.0
	15.0
	20.0
	25.0
	50.0
	100.0
	250.0
	500.0
	1.0K
	2.5K

pc = distance in parsecs

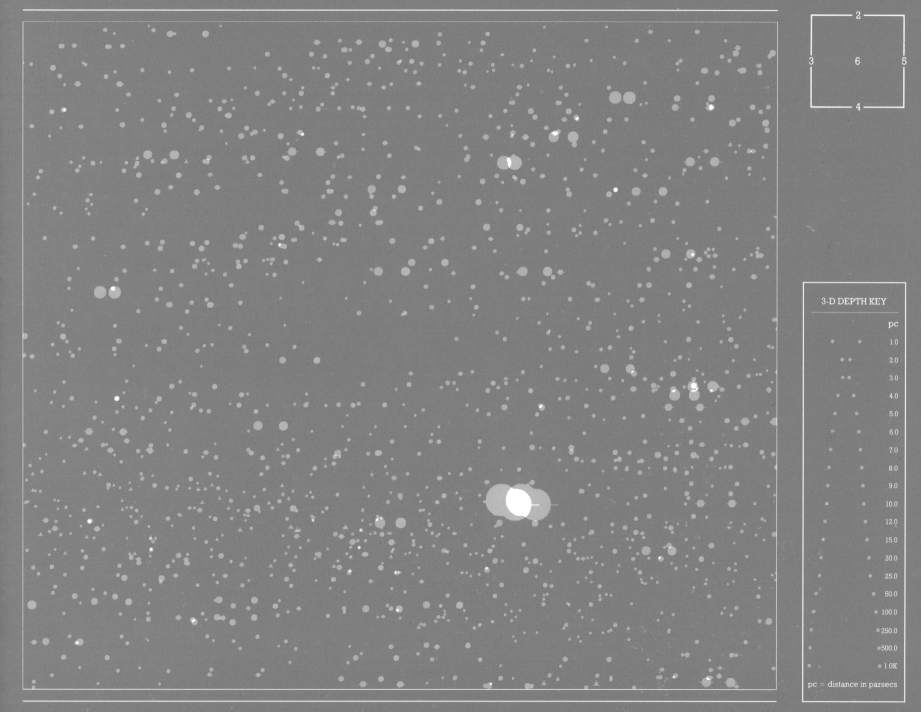

2
3   6   5
4

3-D DEPTH KEY

pc

1.0
2.0
3.0
4.0
5.0
6.0
7.0
8.0
9.0
10.0
12.0
15.0
20.0
25.0
50.0
100.0
250.0
500.0
1.0K

pc = distance in parsecs

travelling. This does not mean that our own galaxy is at the centre of the universe: what it means is that the universe is expanding as a whole, and the observed effects would be the same from whichever galaxy they were seen.

The most favoured explanation for the expanding universe is that it is moving out from an original explosion, the "big bang", which may have taken place between 10,000 million and 20,000 million years ago. Whether this expansion is real, whether it will go on for ever, or whether it will slow down and go into reverse, creating a contracting universe, is uncertain.

One of the difficulties of the big bang theory is that the original explosion might be expected to have produced an even distribution of matter throughout space. On a local scale galaxies do not appear to be distributed smoothly in this way: they appear instead to be "structured" rather like water in soap bubbles, with galaxies distributed around the bubbles, lines of galaxies along the junctions of the bubbles, and clusters of galaxies at the points where several bubbles meet. This "structure", if it exists, may be evolving rather like bubbles on a fermenting pond.

Our own galaxy, the Milky Way, its companion and probably satellite galaxies the Magellanic Clouds (Map 8),

The Local Group appears to be an outlying member of a much larger cluster of galaxies. This is the Virgo cluster (Maps 1 and 4), consisting of about 2,500 observed galaxies at an estimated general distance of 15Mpc. Superclusters, which are not accepted by all astronomers, are thought to be large scale groupings of clusters whose overall expansion (part of the uniform expansion of space) is being slowed down by the braking effect of their mutual gravity. About a dozen possible superclusters are shown as distant groupings on the maps: examples include the Coma Berenices grouping (Maps 1–4) and the Perseus grouping (Map 7). Recent observations have suggested that the Virgo (super)cluster and the Hydra-Centaurus (super)cluster (Map 4) are themselves being braked by a centre of gravity attraction, possibly a truly massive supercluster, which may lie hidden at a distance of about 150Mpc behind the Milky Way in the direction of the Southern Cross.

The distances to galaxies shown on the maps are very much a rough estimation. The scale of distance depends on whether observed redshift is a direct indicator of the rate at with objects are moving apart, and on the calculations whereby that expansion is converted into distance. Even if all the assumptions are correct, the scale may exaggerate or diminish the true distances by more than 50 per cent. The individual movement of galaxies against the background of the uniform expansion of space will mean that many galaxies are wrongly placed against an already uncertain scale. Bearing these factors in mind, the Galaxy Maps show objects out to around 1000Mpc. Galaxies seen over such distances appear as very faint objects, and their light will have taken up to one-fifth of the estimated elapsed age of the universe just to reach us. They may not, however, represent the limit of seeing. Towards the limits of observation appear another class of object, "quasars".

Some of these objects display such enormous redshifts that astronomers have looked for some explanation other than recession velocity. If their redshifts really are a direct indication of distance, then quasars are the most distant and intrinsically luminous objects yet observed, being up to 100 times as bright as giant galaxies, and with the most distant examples approaching the theoretical limits of the observable universe, 3–6Gpc distant, their light having taken most of elapsed time just to reach us. This may mean they are objects observed "before" an eventual transformation into galaxies, or it may mean they are objects quite unlike anything yet known.

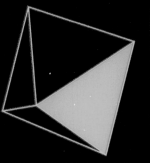

OCTAHEDRON (8 FACES)

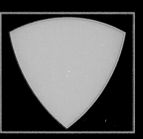

GALAXY MAPS

Galaxy Maps are drawn on octahedrons.

This photograph covers less than 1° of sky towards the centre of the Virgo Cluster. The two main objects are elliptical galaxies: the disc-like objects are spiral galaxies, like the Milky Way.

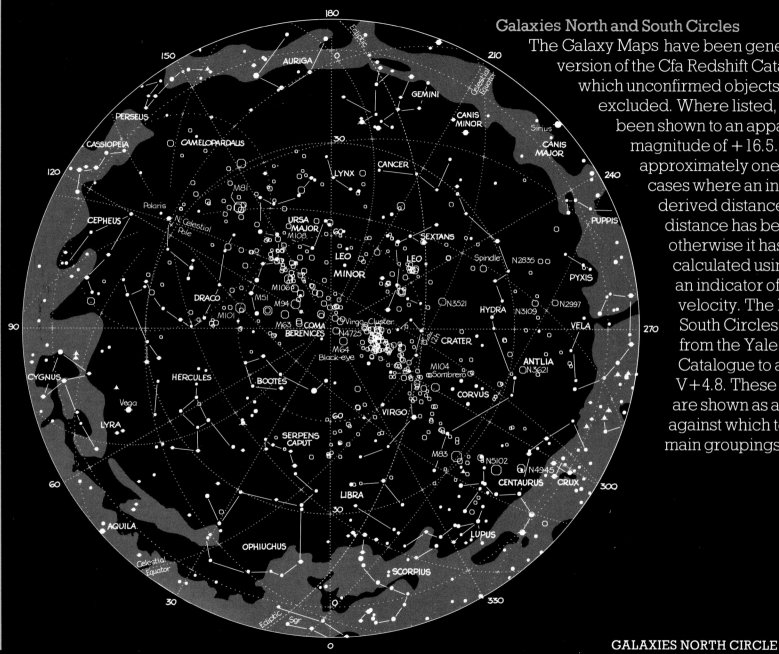

Galaxies North and South Circles

The Galaxy Maps have been generated from a version of the Cfa Redshift Catalogue from which unconfirmed objects have been excluded. Where listed, objects have been shown to an apparent magnitude of +16.5. In the approximately one hundred cases where an independently derived distance is listed, this distance has been used; otherwise it has been calculated using redshift as an indicator of recession velocity. The North and South Circles include stars from the Yale Bright Star Catalogue to a limit of V+4.8. These bright stars are shown as a "foreground" against which to view the main groupings of galaxies.

GALAXIES NORTH CIRCLE

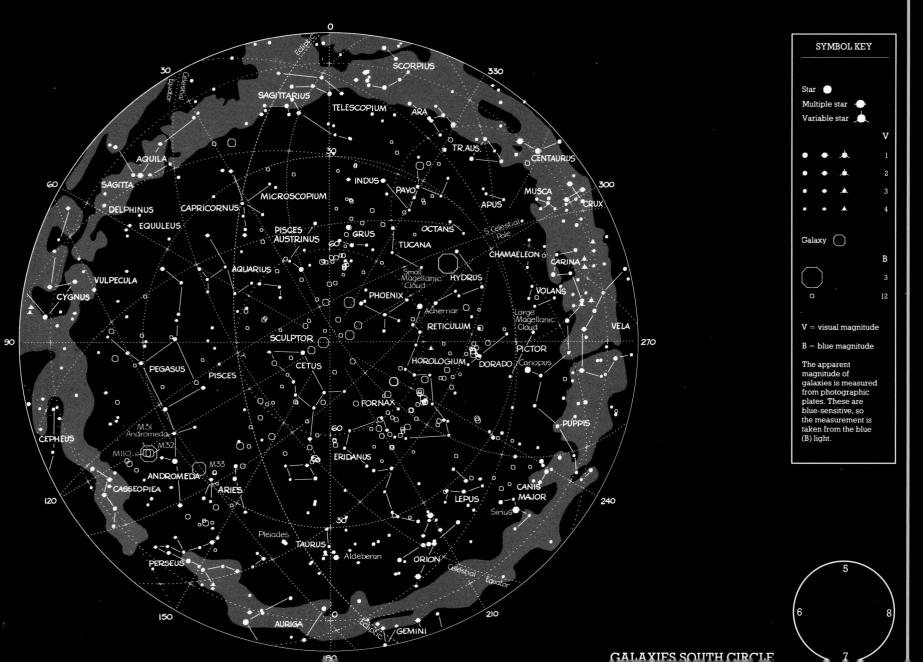

SYMBOL KEY

Star ●

Multiple star ●—

Variable star ●

			V
●	●	▲	1
●	●	▲	2
●	●	▲	3
●	●	▲	4

Galaxy ⬡

	B
⬡	3
▫	12

V = visual magnitude

B = blue magnitude

The apparent magnitude of galaxies is measured from photographic plates. These are blue-sensitive, so the measurement is taken from the blue (B) light.

GALAXIES SOUTH CIRCLE

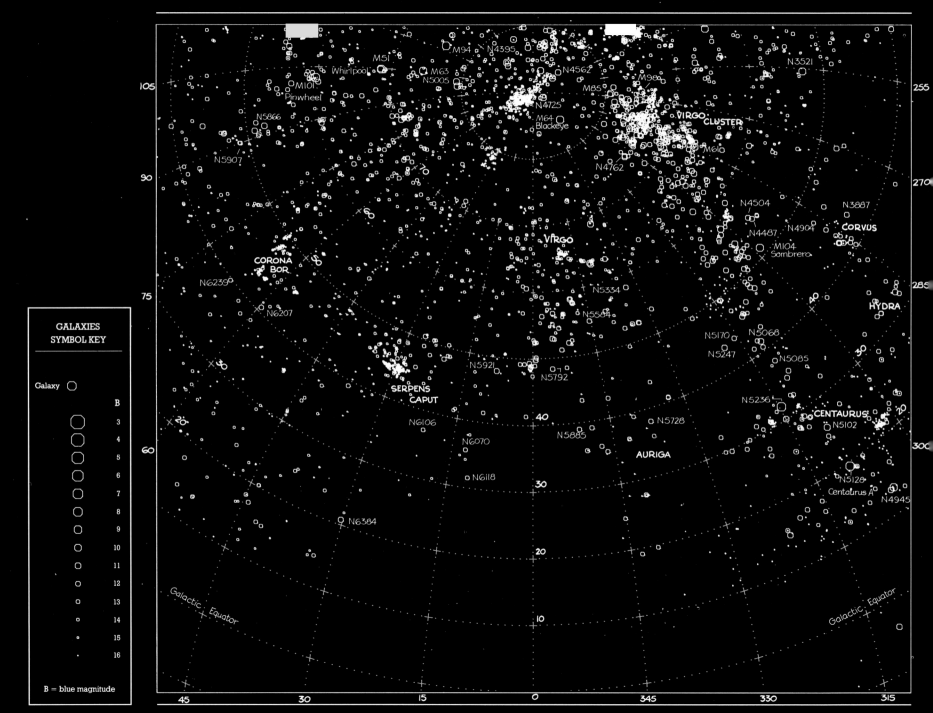

GALAXIES
SYMBOL KEY

Galaxy ○

	B
◯	3
◯	4
◯	5
◯	6
◯	7
◯	8
◯	9
○	10
○	11
○	12
○	13
○	14
○	15
·	16

B = blue magnitude

3-D DEPTH KEY

Mpc

● < 1.0

● 2.5

● 5.0

○ plane
  of   10.0
  page

● 25.0

● 50.0

● 100.0

● 250.0

● 500.0

● 1000.0

● 2500.0

Mpc = distance in
      Mega parsecs

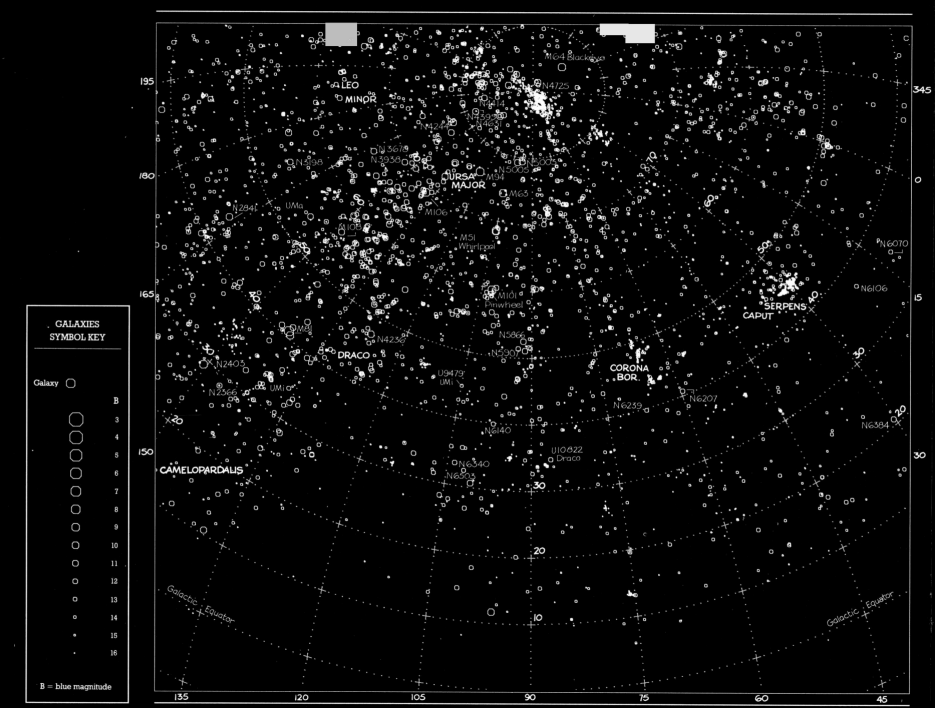

GALAXIES
SYMBOL KEY

		B
Galaxy	○	
	⬡	3
	⬡	4
	⬡	5
	⬡	6
	○	7
	○	8
	○	9
	○	10
	○	11
	○	12
	○	13
	○	14
	○	15
	·	16

B = blue magnitude

3-D DEPTH KEY

Mpc

< 1.0

2.5

5.0

plane
of
page   10.0

25.0

50.0

100.0

250.0

500.0

1000.0

2500.0

Mpc = distance in
Mega parsecs

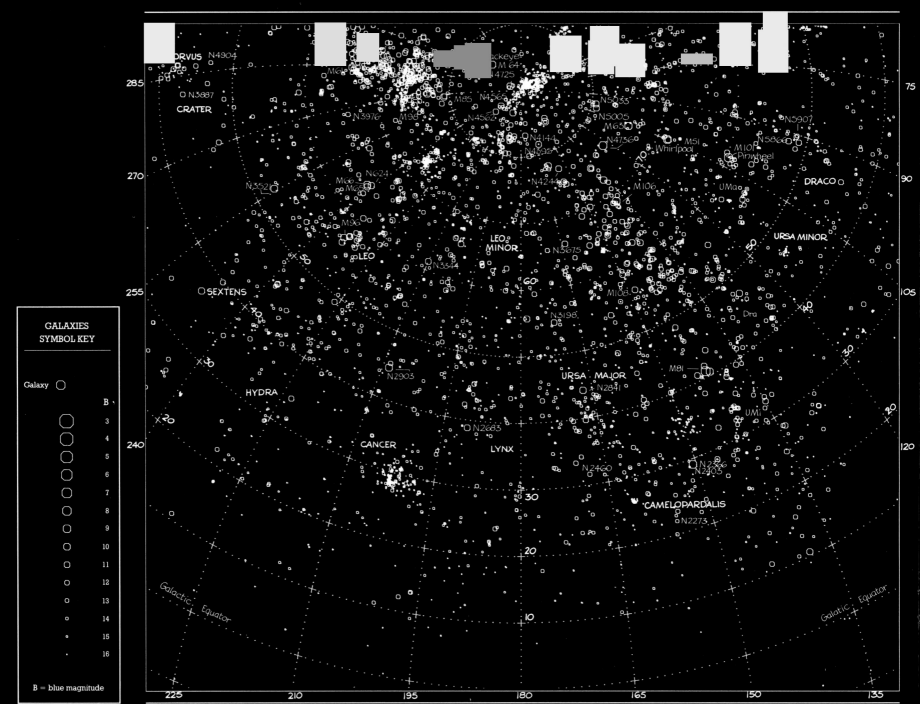

GALAXIES
SYMBOL KEY

Galaxy ○

	B
○	3
○	4
○	5
○	6
○	7
○	8
○	9
○	10
○	11
○	12
○	13
○	14
·	15
·	16

B = blue magnitude

4   2
3
7

3-D DEPTH KEY

Mpc

● < 1.0

2.5

5.0

plane
of
page   10.0

25.0

50.0

100.0

250.0

500.0

1000.0

2500.0

Mpc = distance in
Mega parsecs

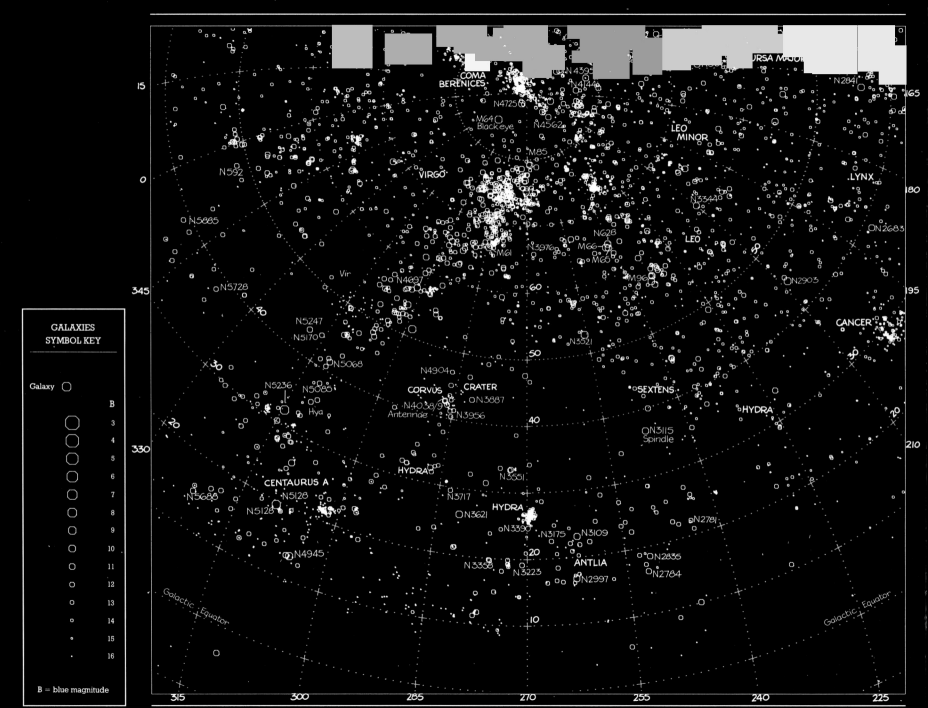

**GALAXIES
SYMBOL KEY**

Galaxy ○

	B
	3
	4
	5
	6
	7
	8
	9
	10
	11
	12
	13
	14
	15
	16

B = blue magnitude

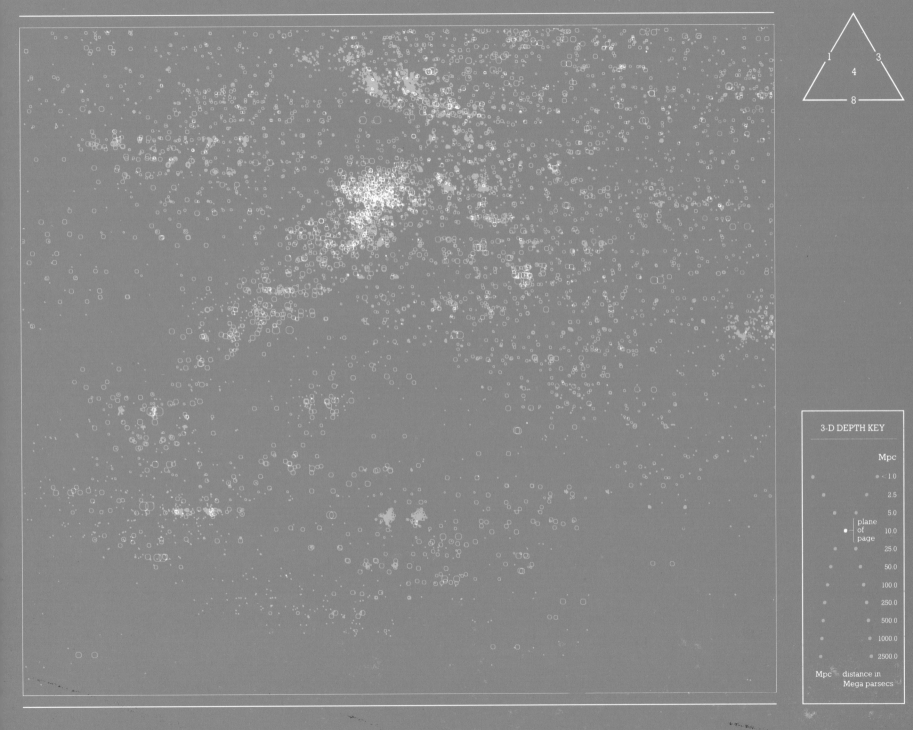

3-D DEPTH KEY

Mpc

● < 1.0

2.5

5.0

plane
of   10.0
page

25.0

50.0

100.0

250.0

500.0

1000.0

2500.0

Mpc = distance in
Mega parsecs

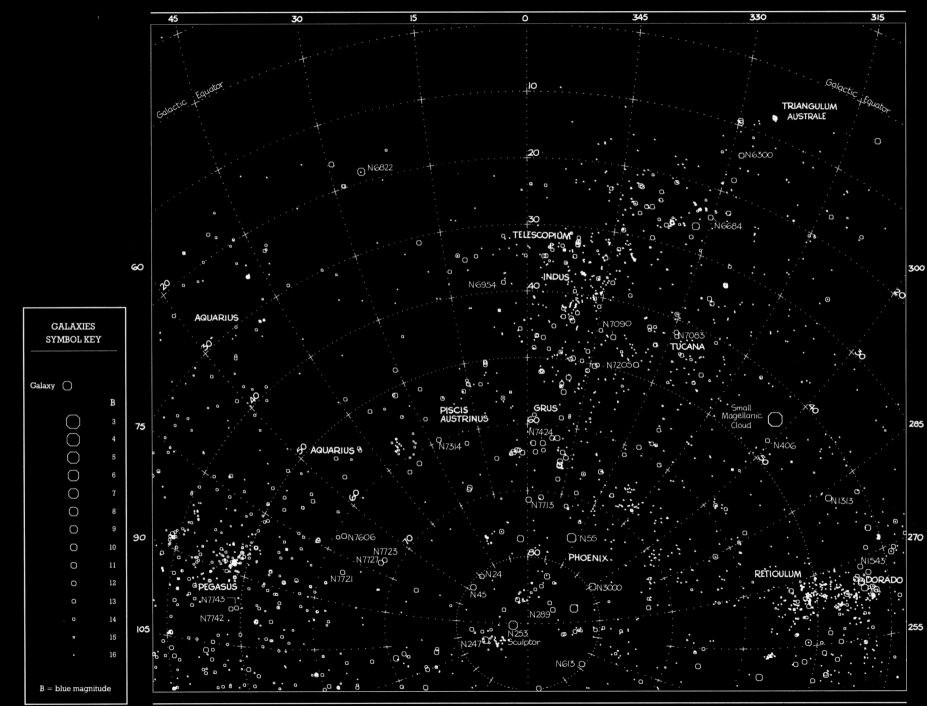

GALAXIES
SYMBOL KEY

Galaxy ◯

	B
◯	3
◯	4
◯	5
◯	6
◯	7
◯	8
◯	9
◯	10
◯	11
◦	12
◦	13
·	14
◦	15
·	16

B = blue magnitude

3-D DEPTH KEY

Mpc

● <1.0

● 2.5

● 5.0

plane
● of   10.0
page

● 25.0

● 50.0

● 100.0

● 250.0

● 500.0

● 1000.0

● 2500.0

Mpc = distance in
Mega parsecs

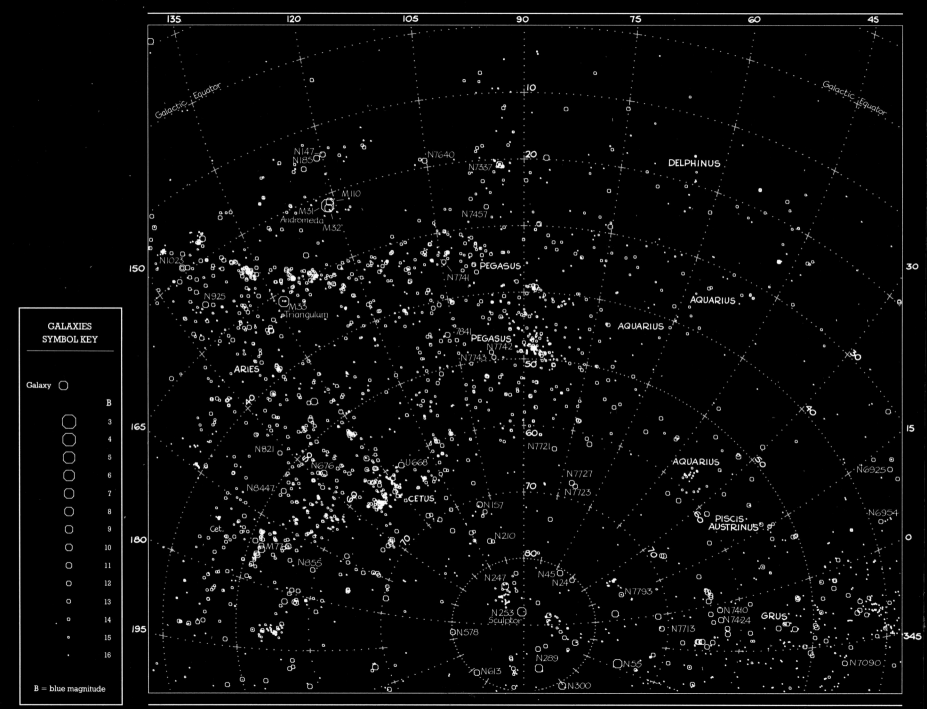

GALAXIES
SYMBOL KEY

Galaxy ⬡

	B
⬡	3
⬡	4
⬡	5
⬡	6
◯	7
◯	8
◯	9
◯	10
◯	11
○	12
○	13
○	14
○	15
·	16

B = blue magnitude

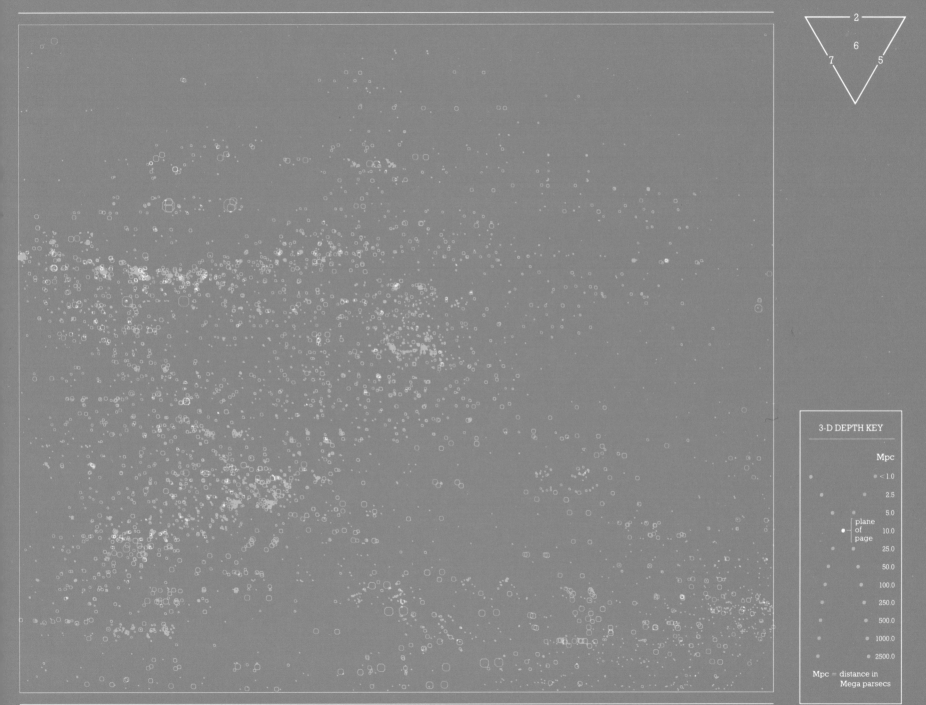

2

6

7   5

3-D DEPTH KEY

Mpc

● < 1.0

● 2.5

● 5.0

● plane
of
page
10.0

● 25.0

● 50.0

● 100.0

● 250.0

● 500.0

● 1000.0

● 2500.0

Mpc = distance in
Mega parsecs

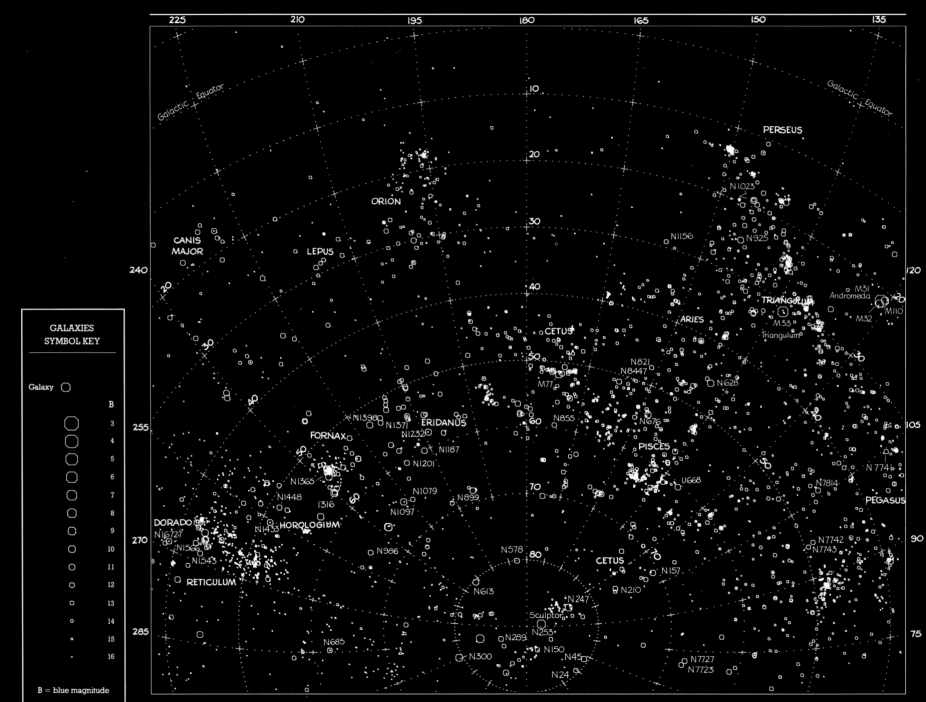

GALAXIES
SYMBOL KEY

Galaxy	◯	
		B
	◯	3
	◯	4
	◯	5
	◯	6
	◯	7
	◯	8
	◯	9
	○	10
	○	11
	○	12
	○	13
	○	14
	·	15
	·	16

B = blue magnitude

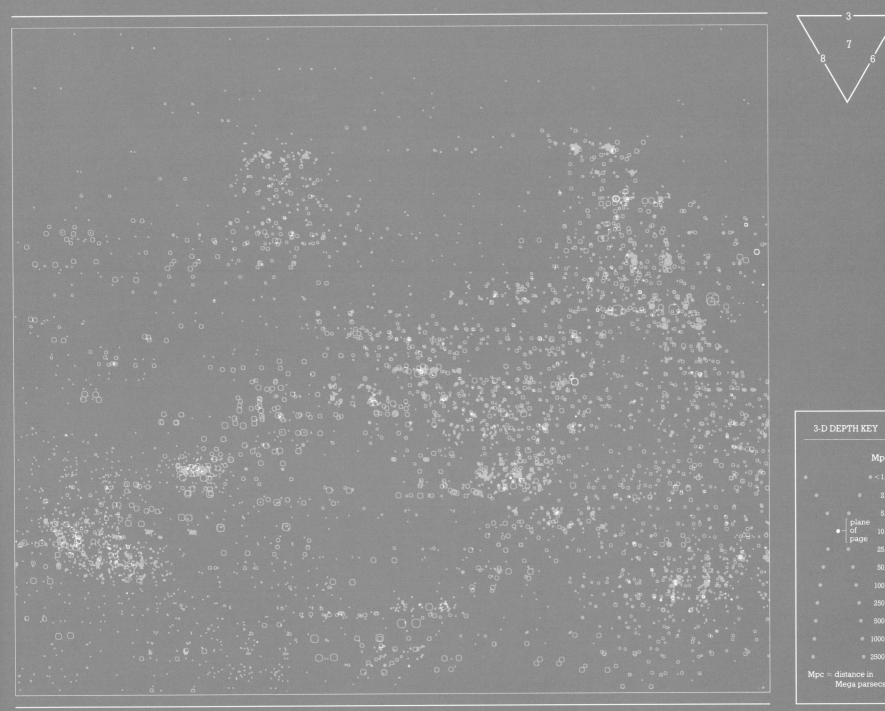

3
7
8   6

3-D DEPTH KEY

Mpc

● < 1.0

2.5

5.0

plane
of   10.0
page

25.0

50.0

100.0

250.0

500.0

1000.0

2500.0

Mpc = distance in
Mega parsecs

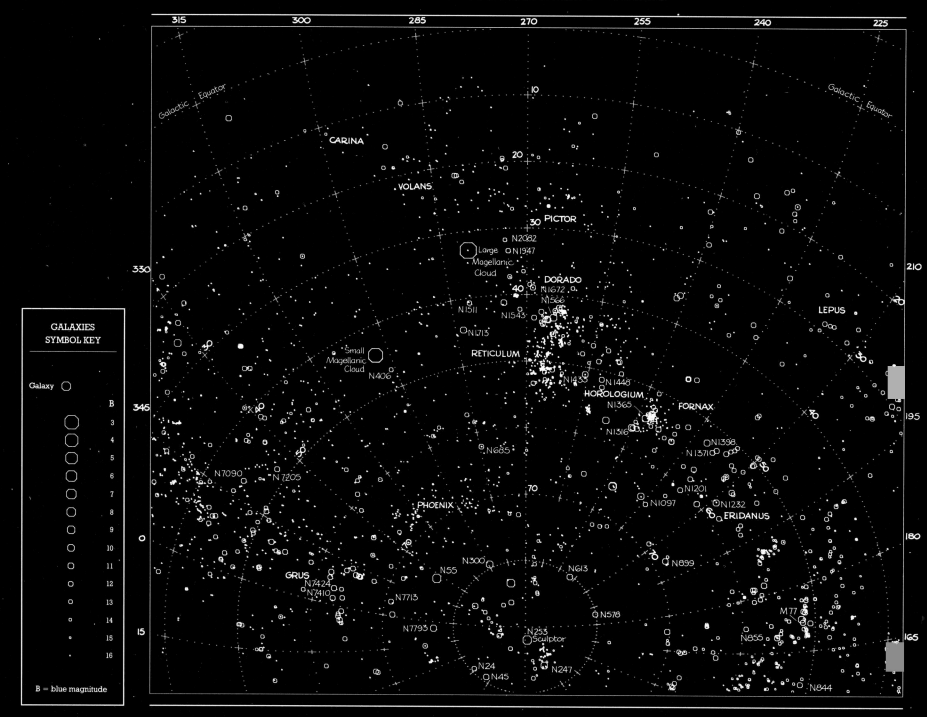

GALAXIES
SYMBOL KEY

Galaxy ◯

	B
◯	3
◯	4
◯	5
◯	6
◯	7
◯	8
◯	9
○	10
○	11
○	12
○	13
○	14
○	15
·	16

B = blue magnitude

3-D DEPTH KEY

Mpc

< 1.0

2.5

5.0

plane
of   10.0
page

25.0

50.0

100.0

250.0

500.0

1000.0

2500.0

Mpc = distance in
        Mega parsecs

Index

Page numbers in *italic* refer to illustrations.

Authors' Acknowledgments

The Authors would like to thank the following individuals and institutions for their help in assembling the database from which this book was prepared: Dr. K.F. Hartley; The Royal Greenwich Observatory; The Royal Astronomical Society; Sandy Leggett; A.C. Davenhall, The Royal Observatory, Edinburgh; Dr. Brian Whitmore; Queen Mary College, London; Dr. D. Hoffleit of the Yale Observatory for permission to use the Yale Bright Star Catalogue; The University of Arizona Press for permission to use data from the New General Catalogue of Non-Stellar Astronomical Objects; Professor Wilhelm Gliese and Dr. Harmut Jahreiss of the Astronomisches Rechen-Institut, Heidelberg for permission to use the Catalogue of Nearby Stars, and Professor John Huchra of the Harvard-Smithsonian Center for Astrophysics for permission to use data from the CfA Redshift Catalogue. The Authors would also like to thank Sue Hall, John Hopkins and James Bracegirdle for their generosity in the loan of machinery, and John Alexander for reading parts of the manuscript. Responsibility for errors remains with the Authors.

Photographic Acknowledgments

John Cox: page 27.

Peter Loughran: page 21.

Richard Monkhouse: pages 30 and 32.

Copyright Royal Observatory, Edinburgh: half title page, title page and pages 10/11, 22 and 25 (right).

Copyright Royal Observatory and Anglo-Australian Telescope Board: pages 8, 11, 10, 23, 24, 25 (left) and 77.